Boomer Boosters:

Inspiration for Aging Baby Boomers

J. J. Ross Johnston

Surrey, B.C.

BOOMER BOOSTERS:

INSPIRATION FOR AGING BABY BOOMERS

Published by Soul Care Sojourners

Surrey, British Columbia

ISBN: 978-1548121624

Dedication

This book is dedicated to the multitude of Baby Boomers and Seniors whom I have had the privilege of knowing and ministering with across the decades. You have all taught me much and inspired my life in untold ways. A special dedication goes to that one Baby Boomer who has been my life partner for 46 years, my dear wife, Beverley! Thank you for your constant faith in me and encouragement through all our seasons of life.

Table of Contents

φ

LET'S BEGIN!

"There is no old age. There is, as there always was, just you." That's Carol Grace's observation on life.[1] Most people who have reached the senior years do not think of themselves as senior. Oliver Wendell Homes concluded that "Old age is fifteen years older than I am."[2] But the years do relentlessly march by. We cannot believe how fast time has flown. Life is like the grass that quickly withers said the Psalmist of the Bible. Where indeed, have the years gone?!

Yet, in the seeming quick passage of time, a full life has been lived and many lessons have been learned from challenges faced day to day. How are those teachings to carry us in the latter half of life? In reflection, this baby boomer has recorded some of his own adventures (and misadventures). The lessons learned may bring hope and encouragement to others; maybe even, to you. As a baby boomer, I am far from alone. Further, we face the latter years somewhat differently to earlier generations.

Baby boomers are the demographic group born during the post-World War II baby boom, approximately between the years 1946 and 1964. This sizeable population group has moved through society like a balloon passing through a garden hose. Now we are reaching the senior years. Every day, 10,000 boomers turn 65! But they are not going quietly off into the twilight. "76 million American children were born between 1946 and 1964, representing a cohort that is significant on account of its size alone. In 2004, the British baby boomers held 80% of the UK's wealth and bought 80% of all top of the range cars, 80% of cruises and 50% of skincare products."[3] They don't plan to slow down this active, privileged

1

lifestyle because of having reached the traditional "retirement age." Watch out world! Boomers intend to stay on top. However, we haven't been this way before so we are actively figuring out where to go and how to get there even as we are aging.

My wife gave me a new GPS for Christmas. It's fun to use, even when I know where I am going. When I know my destination I often take routes other than the one set out by the GPS. When I do, the message comes up: "Recalculating direction, 20%, 50%, 70%, 92%" ... and a new course is chosen. We frequently do that in life. As we age we repeatedly recalculate our direction. For baby boomers entering the second half, or third, third of life, this is even more true. Boomers born between the years 1946 and 1964, are now in their early 50's through 70's. They are already "seniors" or soon to be considered so. This reality forces a recalculation in thinking. It is a special season in life. This book is composed of random thoughts – a potpourri, if you will – of one Boomer's reflections on the transitions, challenges and special joys of these seasons of life. If you are one of us, may you find these writings uplifting, hopeful and encouraging for what you are facing. If you are not there yet, your turn is coming! Let this help prepare you with a positive outlook on what is ahead. If you are already past your seventies and in an older season, there will be encouragement here for you too.

My parents, Kent and Eldene, had what I consider to be, a unique romance. My Dad had lived on the same farm in rural, "back woods" Ontario (about 65 miles northwest of Toronto) that he was moved onto in 1917 when he was six months old. He and my Grandfather were bachelor farmers on this farm in 1948. My Mom, born in Toronto, had moved with her family to Michigan when she was thirteen, and from there a couple of years later, to New York City. That's where she grew up to work in a famous research institute. One summer she and her mother travelled back to my grandmother's home area not far from my father's farm. Due to the connection of mutual relatives they ended up visiting the Johnston farm one warm summer's day. When they arrived, the men were working out in the fields. The women decided to wait for them until they came in for supper. Doors were never locked in that time and place, so they went into the farmhouse to wait. Now remember, this was the home of two bachelors. Upon entry, these two women set to work cleaning house and preparing a scrumptious meal. When the men finally came in, for my Dad it was "love at first bite!"

Love struck, these two young adults began a letter and occasional visit relationship across the almost 500 miles separating them. On February 19, 1949, they were married at Bedford Park Presbyterian Church in The Bronx area of New York City. From downtown Manhattan, my mother moved to this remote snow-covered farm to live with her new husband. I don't think she ever recovered! It was the reality version of TV's "Green Acres," starring Eva Gabor and Eddie Albert, brought to life! From the day she arrived, my Mom could not wait to move off the farm. She did ... about 40 years later! In spite of occasional strong vocal disagreements and financial hardships she made the best of her new circumstances. They gave birth to five children and stayed together in that marriage for 57 years until my Dad's death in 2006. The major lesson they modelled for us, was that no matter how tough things got, you stick together 'until death do you part.'

In 1950, I was the first-born to this intrepid couple. Yes, in the vernacular of my kids, in those "olden days" I attended a one-room country schoolhouse for my elementary years. After high school in a nearby town I went on to do graduate and post-graduate studies in Winnipeg, Kansas City and eventually completed my doctoral degree in California the month before turning sixty. I pastored or served in ministry settings during or between my study years, for almost forty years. In my last pastoral setting of over six years, I ministered to seniors (50+) at a large church in southwestern British Columbia, Canada. When I commenced that ministry, the people helped me celebrate my 60th birthday with 60 gifts and 60 items in each gift! What fun that day was!

My wife, Bev, and I came into that ministry setting with a life-long love for older adults. When in seminary in Kansas City,

Missouri, at 24-years-of-age I taught the senior adult class (the Bereans) in the church we attended. We fell in love with all of them during those four years and have continued to love seniors since then. What a blessed surprise came to us to learn 22 years after our leaving that group, that remaining members of the Berean class had gathered to have a special time of prayer for us when we were going through a challenging time in pastoral ministry! Wow! There is such power in the relational bonds that are forged. We have experienced the same in all our other settings of service. This is the background and context out of which come these reflections. My hope is that they will provide some inspiration and encouragement to baby boomers and older seniors going through this season of life. Never having been this old before, it's hard to know how to do it right!

φ

Chapter 1

WORTHLESSNESS AND DISCOURAGEMENT

Are You Feeling Like You've Been Kicked Around? Forsaken?

For some aging adults, the growing old experience feels like a big negative. For others who embrace a positive attitude, aging becomes a daily unfolding of new adventures. Personal choices and life circumstances impact us all. Are you one who feels like you've been kicked around? Forsaken?

I love the Psalmist of the Bible for one primary reason. He felt every emotion I've ever felt, experienced every human experience I've ever lived and he wrote about them all with powerful insight! No matter what I've encountered that totally stressed me out, it seems the Psalmist had also been there at some point in his life and left us godly wisdom for dealing with it.

Now there are some extremities I haven't been pushed to as yet. For example, his harassment recorded in Psalm 56:1-2: *1 Take my side, God – I'm getting kicked around, stomped on every day. 2 Not a day goes by but somebody beats me up; They make it their duty to beat me up (The Message)4* I've had some tough days, but none that bad! Yet in response he does the best thing possible: *3 When I get really afraid I come to you in trust.* This I have done many times!

And yet, are there not times when we feel like we can take no more? We think we are all alone, seemingly forgotten, even by God.

Have we not all had those Job-like seasons when it seems one setback is piled upon another and another? Have you been there? Are you there now? What are we to do?! Let's do the same thing the Psalmist did. Let's turn to the truth about our loving God. He reveals it in verse 8: *You've kept track of my every toss and turn through the sleepless nights, Each tear entered in your ledger, each ache written in your book (The Message).*

Think of it. God not only knows the number of hairs on each of our heads (a number that changes daily, if not hourly, by the way!), but he keeps track of every tear we shed, every ache we feel, every toss and turn we make through sleepless nights. He records them all. He knows! He cares. Can you picture God gently stroking your brow while counting each tear, whispering "There, there child, it's alright," just as would a loving mother? That is the reality!

And so, how are we to respond? In the words of Max Lucado: "His kingdom needs you. The poor need you; the lonely need you; the church needs you ... the cause of God needs you. You are part of *'the overall purpose he is working out in everything and everyone'* (Eph. 1:11, *MSG*). The kingdom needs you to discover and deploy your unique skill. Use it to ... get the word out. God is with us; we are not alone".5 Some unnamed person said, "It will all be okay in the end. So, if it's not all okay, that means you are not yet at the end!" Hm-m-m. I like that.

Feel better now? Excuse me. I've got to go. The pity party is over. It's time to get back to work for Him!

Not Forgotten!

Has God forgotten you? As a child, I attended a one-room, red-bricked school house located one mile from our farm home. In our most populous year we had a student enrollment of 21 – in all eight grades! My largest class ever was five, but for most years there were only two of us in our grade. Sometimes I feel like such a relic! Nowadays a class of 21 would seem small. However, consider the challenge for the teacher then of each day having to prepare and give lessons for all eight grades! One of the forbidden things we students occasionally did at recess or lunch hour, was to carve our initials on the exterior bricks of the building. Yes, we did get in trouble for it, if caught! I have a mental image of my initials, RJ, deeply carved in one such brick. It has been almost 60 years since I graduated from Grade 8 and left that school. Yet, if I were to go back to that building, now a remodeled weekend home for some folks from 'the City' (i.e., Toronto), I know I would find my initials still embedded there. Decades have passed, but my old school still "remembers" me!

Adversity in life can leave us feeling forsaken, forgotten, forlorn and without hope. Are you living at that address? At our deepest depths, we can even think that God doesn't care. I understand how one can arrive at this location. Long sieges with illness, wearying vigils, then the death of a precious loved one whom we have prayed for and whose life we fought for, month after month, may bring us to a point of seeming abandonment – even by God Himself. Or maybe it's the daily struggle for financial survival with repeated unexpected financial hits, seeming never to get ahead and often barely surviving, that leaves us exhausted, hopeless and ready to quit. You pray, but in despair think that God is not even listening. It's so hopeless.

May I propose an alternate view for you? It comes from Isaiah 49:16. The God who does love you, says: *"See, I have engraved you on the palms of my hands; your walls are ever before me."*[6] Really?! Can this be true? Your name is engraved on His hands?

Like my initials permanently embedded in that school brick, still there almost six decades later, God is saying your name is engraved (today, we might think, tattooed) on His hands? How many times a day do you use your hands? Look at your hands (as I am now doing as I type this)? See them in front of you? God is saying, that is how often I see and think of you. All day long! And when He says "your walls are ever before me" He was referring to the walls of Jerusalem which at that time lay in ruins. He is reminding His people that he was fully aware of the state of Zion's walls and that He had a plan to rebuild them, which came about under Nehemiah's leadership. His city was not forgotten. And neither are you. Take courage dear friend. God has not forgotten you.

Do you need one more word of uplift to bring this home? Here it is, from *The Living Bible* translation: *"How precious it is, Lord, to realize that you are thinking about me constantly! I can't even count how many times in a day your thoughts turn towards me. And when I waken in the morning, you are still thinking of me!"* (Psalm 139:17-18, LB). I should make another trip back to my old school and look for my initials. I know they will still be there. And I know your name is engraved on God's palms and he is thinking of you – right now.

Discouragement or Hope?

I am inspired by the attitude of the Apostle Paul found in Romans 15:13: Oh! May the God of green hope fill you up with joy, fill you up with peace, so that your believing lives, filled with the life-giving energy of the Holy Spirit, will brim over with hope! (The Message)

It is in great contrast to that of the Psalmist found in Psalm 42:5,11:

Why are you down in the dumps, dear soul?

Why are you crying the blues?

Fix my eyes on God

soon I'll be praising again. (The Message)

Or in the more familiar words of the New International Version it reads:

Why are you downcast, O my soul?

Why so disturbed within me?

Put your hope in God,

for I will yet praise him, my Savior and my God.

This leads me to ask: which most closely matches the position you are in at this season of aging? It is easy to become discouraged, feel flat and uninspired. How can we turn that around?

What is needed, is hope. "Hope is miracle medicine!" One of my former seminary profs, Mendell Taylor, wrote in a devotional book, "When our hope is limited we quickly give in to discouragement. This leads to a shortage of long-suffering, and brings a series of spiritual problems: (1) We become cold – the fires of hope cool down until we are left with a meaningless routine. (2) We become critical – everything strikes us the wrong way: we quickly and impulsively register a protest of our dislikes. (3) We become cliquish – drifting into the social circle of those of like spiritual dwarfism; under the guise of mutual friendship, we bring

9

out the worst in each other. Overwhelmed by this avalanche of defeats, long-suffering dies."[7]

This sounds deadly. When feeling slightly depressed or discouraged – and I'm not referring to clinical depression here, which is far more serious and may need competent medical treatment – but depression that is the result of setbacks and difficulties – when feeling this way, we are called to put our hope in God and to praise Him for who He is! When we do, God will meet our needs and through us, the needs of others. But it must be God in us. We can't do it on our own.

How do we find this focus that will get us on course for the New Year? A quote from Randall Hunter in his book, *Wisdom Hunter*, seems like good guidance for us. He said: **"Let God have your life, let wisdom guide your life, and let people be your life."**[8] This focus should get us on our hopeful way once more. But how can we actualize it? Here's an idea that might be helpful, shared by Elizabeth Newehuyse:

"My husband and I like to play "what if?" We sit and toss out ideas: What if we moved out of state? What if we enclosed our porch? What if we got a dog? Some of the what ifs come to fruition; others don't. But we've found that the very process airs out our marriage, opens doors and windows of possibility, draws us closer. It's not an idle exercise; to dream, to crack open that door, starts things happening."[9]

Find someone to play this "what if" game with, set your focus as indicated and discover green hope to guide you through the days ahead!

Φ

Chapter 2

THE THIRD THIRD – FINISHING WELL

The Third Third

Some refer to the senior years of life as the 'second half.' However, others talk about this being the 'third third' of life. Richard and Shirley Bergstrom in their great book, *Third Calling*, describe it this way. "We define stages in life as: First Calling – the challenges of young adulthood; Second Calling – the responsibilities of midlife; and Third Calling – the opportunities of maturity. It's a new stage, a blank canvas we can fill with color, action and story. It is time to engage in our Third Calling."[10] Given the average extension of life in the western world, many seniors can expect to live life in retirement for as long, or longer than the span of their working careers. This begs the question, "What am I going to do with this third third of my life that I may be graced to live? How will I remain productive for the common good?"

A gerontologist who has focused on these kinds of issues has prepared a book and DVD study entitled *Even Better After 50: How to Become (and Remain) Well of Body, Wise of Mind, and Whole of Spirit in the Second Half of Life*. This is one of the many resources offered by Dr. Richard Johnson through his institute on aging.[11]

At the heart of this focus is a desire to live life well before God no matter what our age. For many baby boomers, the so-called "retirement years" loom large. Some are just now entering in while others know they need to soon start thinking about it. How does one prepare? It's a great question with no one simple answer.

An observation by Dr. James Houston, first principal at Regent College, Vancouver, got my mind to thinking. This very much alive and engaged then 89-year-old published a book, co-authored with Michael Parker, entitled *A Vision for the Aging Church: Renewing Ministry for and by Seniors*.[12] One of their findings, he reported, is that with extended life spans and improved health the era of the sixties is no longer viewed as time to wind up one's work career and contribution and commence to wind down one's life. Rather, the sixties are now viewed as the era in which folks re-evaluate goals, skills, resources and determine what their career and contribution will be for the final third of their lives. It is not at all a winding up but rather a shifting to new frontiers to conquer for a new era of impact.

Wow! That is exciting. Is this how you view the last third of your life? Or, if you are already in it, is this what you are experiencing? It's actually not a new approach. The apostle Paul had this attitude. *"13 But one thing I do: Forgetting what is behind and straining toward what is ahead, 14 I press on toward the goal to win the prize for which God has called me heavenward in Christ Jesus. 15 All of us, then, who are mature should take such a view of things."* Obviously, he wasn't done living. He had work to do up to his very last breath.

What am I going to do in my final third of life? God is stirring me to try some new things and to set some new goals for service and ministry. There's a lot of life left to live. I recently found a new hero. He's not someone I personally know but read about in a news report. A pastor in a denomination of which I used to be a member, the report stated that after 27 years in his last church an official retirement party had been held to honor him – at age 92! Alright! I have a new goal now! As long as I have breath there is ministry to do – not only for me but also for you!

"Seasoned Citizens"

The season of life known as 'the senior years' is often viewed in a negative light in North American culture. It is seen as a time of loss and diminishment – something to be feared, not embraced. This is not God's view of seniors! In fact, here is what God commands in Leviticus 19:32: *"Rise in the presence of the aged, show respect for the elderly and revere your God. I am the LORD."* We are commanded to respect the elderly in the same sentence that we are told to reverence God. In his book, *The Joys of Aging* (1988), Martin A. Janis[13] captured this attitude in several comments I want to share with you. These are not "senior citizens" but, "seasoned citizens"!! I like that. He goes on to identify several truths about seasoned citizens.

If you're not learning, you're not growing and if you're not growing, you're not living (you're dying!). The opposite of growing (which is harder) is "withering" (which is easier!!) (p.44,88). "I believe older persons can and should change. If you're not learning, you're not growing ... I also believe that growth is enhanced by a positive outlook, laced with a good sense of humor" (p.88). Norman Cousins says everyone "must convince the elderly that the way they look at old age is crucial to their youth and productivity" (p.34). Hamlet said:

> *"To be, or not to be, that is the question,*
>
> *Whether 'tis nobler in the mind to suffer*
>
> *The slings and arrows of outrageous fortune,*
>
> *Or to take arms against a sea of troubles,*
>
> *And by opposing end them"* (p.26).

Robert Browning in his poem, "Rabbi Ben Ezra," invited us to:

> *"Grow old along with me!*
>
> *The best is yet to be,*
>
> *The last of life, for which the first was made:*

Our times are in His hand.

Who saith, 'A whole I planned,

Youth shows but half; trust God: see all,

nor be afraid'" (p.53)!

We must begin to see "retirement" as our "renewal period," said Janis. "The retirement years, it seems to me, can be like a second spring, which, in fact, does occur in nature each autumn. It is a time when the heavy heat and humidity of summer give way to mellow sunlight and warm days and cooler, earlier evenings. Roses bloom anew, as do the fall flowers and new-planted grasses. So, let's compare these years to the second spring of autumn and call them the *renewal years*. Or, better yet, the *self*-renewal years" (p.41). Remember that "Good health is found in motion" – "Running water does not stagnate" (p.71).

"Last, but certainly not least, we also need to keep our souls in motion. For our soul, or the spirit, is of equal importance to the body and mind. Spiritual 'motion' must be maintained, as well as the motion of body and mind. Plato said we should never attempt to look after the body without looking after the soul" (p.76-77). Is this enough to mull on for now? I think so. At least it is for me. Happy mulling, seasoned citizens!

To the Finish

For North American football fans, Super Bowl XLIX was a thrilling match. The last play of the game in the final few seconds reversed the direction of a closely fought battle, snatching away sure defeat from the hands of seeming victory. The New England Patriots maintained their four-point lead over the Seahawks with Seattle on the one-yard line and three plays to spare to claim a touchdown win. It was not to be. What a victory for New England quarterback, Tom Brady. What a deflating loss for Russell Wilson. He must have felt crushed. How does a man go on after such a high-visibility failure? Those were my thoughts as I beheld the sad end for the team for which I had been rooting.

It is "only a game" I realize – although a mighty high-priced one, to be sure. Yet there are parallels to what might be called "real life" – the defeats daily faced by so many ordinary people. For one it may be that lost job the whole family counted on for survival and with no seeming prospects for the future. For another it may be the end of all possible treatments for the terminal illness which now leaves only limited days to live. For an older one it may be the forced retirement, feeling they had never achieved the potential or career outcomes expected or desired. Such defeats come in a multitude of forms. After the game ends, how do we go on?

The Apostle Paul had an encouraging word for us. He said, "It's not over until it's over!" Well, those weren't his exact words. What he actually said was: *"But none of these things move me"* (KJV). *"I consider my life worth nothing to me; my only aim is to finish the race and complete the task the Lord Jesus has given me—the task of testifying to the good news of God's grace"* (Acts 20:24). Paul suffered multiplied defeats in his lifetime. Persecution, floggings, shipwreck, being run out of town, imprisonments and riots, to name only a few. Yet he pressed on. His goal was to finish well the race of his life, completing the ministry God had given to him – that of sharing the glorious good news of the gospel of Jesus Christ and His grace. Until his last breath, he fought to finish well.

Russell Wilson, the losing Seattle quarterback should have years yet to play. He tweeted: "At 26 years old I won't allow 1 play or 1 moment define my career." This defeat was not the finish. "We'll be back," he said. Another season. More games. Who knows? Maybe a future Super Bowl opportunity? That's the right attitude.

I know the feeling of loss, of unexpected defeat. I played hard in the game of life. I worked diligently in the ministry to which God called me. Yet an end came. Forced change followed. But I could not quit. I hadn't finished yet. After each defeat, God opened new doors that I stepped through. More wins followed. More people touched for God's kingdom. More fruit in which to rejoice. I thank God for His grace. The choice to press on, however, is our decision. No matter what your defeats of the past, as long as you have breath left, you are not finished. Don't quit. Don't give up your dreams. Don't abandon the ministry God has called you to. Press on ... to the finish.

Retirement

Retirement. Whatcha' gonna do after you do? Retire, that is. Many of you already have. For others, it lies ahead. These interesting findings give some perspective to this life stage decision.

"Research shows that the more physically demanding and less intellectually stimulating an occupation, the sooner the worker will choose to retire, provided he or she can afford it. Judges, politicians, musicians and composers, religious workers, and college professors are among those who tend to stay in their jobs as long as they can. A lawyer or judge is seven times more likely to continue working past sixty-five than the average laborer. Now that mandatory retirement has ended, more and more workers are questioning when to retire or whether they should retire at all."[14]

A definition of "retirement" states it is a noun meaning: "1. The action or fact of leaving one's job and ceasing to work; 2. The period of one's life after leaving one's job and ceasing to work." "Ceasing to work?!" Now there's a misnomer. Most retirees I know work just as hard, or harder, than they ever did in a formal job. Perhaps the difference is that now they are doing more of what they choose to do, or do it for love of family, God and others, and not so much what they once were required to do by an employer. An observation to be made is that retirement will tend to look different for each individual. Some of us who love what we do cannot foresee retiring from it and we intend to always serve in ministry in one form or another, whether paid (hopefully), or unpaid. For others, whose work had been physically demanding, less stimulating or plain boring, retirement may be anticipated as a long-awaited reprieve and release to do things of greater interest. For all, liberation from attendance at a required job frees up hours of time. Unlimited choices await as to how one will now invest the time, health and energy in the years of life remaining. Financial resources may limit some choices, yet there is still so much one may decide to do in retirement.

One of the greatest time commitments may be investment of oneself in the lives of children, grandchildren or great-grandchildren: loving them, mentoring them, leaving to them a legacy. One of our summer highlights is a week spent camping by a lake with three precious granddaughters (now aged 4, 6 and 8). What great times we have bonding with them and building early memories we trust will last their lifetime! We also had the privilege this past summer of journeying to Barkerville, B.C.[15] and revisiting some of the history of our great province. What delightful breaks these were from our normal routine. I hope you too have some renewing times this summer.

Commitment in serving others will bring huge fulfillment in retirement years. The opportunities are endless. What a powerhouse is this great cadre of retired volunteers. Daily they make an indispensable difference in others' lives. So whatcha' gonna do? Retire well! And never cease to work hard and work well! Why retire when you can re-enlist?!

Grandparenting Impressions

My grandparents have been gone from earth a long time. Now in my mid-sixties, I find myself one of them: a grandpa. Some memories of them still impact me. I grew up on the farm that my aging grandfather farmed with my father. Farming is hard work that demands long hours. Yet I remember my Grandpa Joe taking time to show us how to carve a whistle (one that really worked!) from a willow branch. Grandparents must be people who take time for little ones.

My maternal grandfather came to live with us after suffering a stroke in his mid-sixties. His long-term memory was great but his short-term memory was not. Over and over he would ask us what day it was and why he was there. But he would also share his wisdom with us, albeit frequently repeating many of the same sayings or stories. Funny thing though. Some of those truisms have stuck with me for my whole life and served me well. Things like: "You can fool some of the people some of the time and you can fool all of the people some of the time. But, you can't fool all of the people, all of the time." I've lived long enough to observe just how true this is. As a fifteen-year-old teen, I had the privilege, after summoning up all my courage, of asking my Grandpa Turner on his hospital death bed if he had prayed to invite Jesus Christ into his heart to be his Savior. I experienced the joy of leading him in praying the sinner's prayer of confession of sin and receiving, by faith, God's free gift of forgiveness and eternal life. I look forward to seeing my Grandpa again in heaven one day.

I think my favorite grandparent was my maternal grandmother. She lived almost 500 miles away near New York City, but would get into her big old car and drive all the way north to visit us on our remote farm. She always brought gifts! Gifts and big warm hugs and slobbery kisses! How we loved visits from our Grandma. When she came, she filled our lives with good cheer, sunshine, smiles and humor. What a legacy to have left behind!

19

I don't know what Grandma may have expected when we went to visit her. I heard about a grandmother who was giving directions to her grown grandson who was coming to visit with his wife. "You come to the front door of the apartment. I am in apartment 301. There is a big panel at the front door. With your elbow, push button 301. I will buzz you in. Come inside. The elevator is on the right. Get in, and with your elbow push 3. When you get out, I'm on the left. With your elbow, hit my doorbell." "Grandma, replied the grandson, "that sounds easy, but, why am I hitting all these buttons with my elbow?" "What?!" said Grandma. "You coming empty handed?"

As grandparents, we have the privilege of leaving life-long impressions on our precious grandchildren. Memories of love, warmth, humor, encouragement, good cheer or thoughtful gifts may long outlive us. At the same time, who knows the impact grandchildren may have on us? They might even make an eternal difference in some of our lives!

An Axe-Wielding Granny!

My sister, cousin and I were recently laughing (via Facebook) about a memory from our young lives. My Grandma, newly arrived for a visit at our family farm from her home in New York City, undertook to prepare supper for everyone ... from scratch ... literally. Grabbing an axe, she went in search of a free-range chicken digging nearby in the dirt. Chasing it, grabbing it by the legs, all the while with a huge grin on her face, she hauled it over to a chopping block and whacked its head off in one clean motion. Letting go of the unfortunate critter to allow it to die in dignity, to our surprise the headless fowl leapt up and began running around briefly until its expiry. Thereupon Grandma quickly began plucking it, cleaning it and soon had it prepared for a roasting pan to cook in time to be served for supper that night to our family, her sister and her children, my cousins. My grandmother's citified surroundings had not inhibited her in any way from dealing with the needed task at hand, which she accomplished with much laughter and good humor. I can still picture the smiles on her face and hear them in her voice.

The memory stirred in us was of our Grandmother's *joie de vivre* – joy of living. Filled with enthusiasm, she lived her life to the full with much mirth and many smiles. She concurred with an unknown author who noted, "It's important to have a twinkle in your wrinkle!" I know Grandma faced tough times. One such was the mysterious drowning death of her youngest son. Yet overall, happiness characterized her and spilled over on others – and on us whenever she came to visit.

In contrast was another older family relation of my parents whom we would sometimes visit when we were children. His wife was a kind and gentle soul – remarkably. But he was a brusque, cantankerous old curmudgeon whom we feared. Indeed, before every visit we were warned to be on our best behavior and not to upset this man. I remember no smiles on his face. It did not take much to offend him and soon we had very personal memories of the fear he inspired!

Isn't that amazing? Totally opposite memories from two completely differing family members lingering these six-plus decades later? Which pushes me to ask myself some disturbing questions: "What will be the long-term memories and model I am now implanting in my three precious granddaughters and in others who know me? Will they be inspired and encouraged decades from now as they recall vignettes from my life? What about from yours?" I am now the approximate age that my grandmother was when she inspired this memory of the humor of an axe-wielding Granny! Daily my life has a similar influence, modeling for and inspiring those younger around me. As do you. May we encourage and bring good humor to their lives – and provide uplifting memories that will linger in them for decades to come. By the way, the above-mentioned sister and cousin are certainly inspirations to me. They too make me laugh!

Mothers & Grandmothers

May is the month when North Americans celebrate mothers. The second Sunday is Mother's Day. It affords a time for all children to express appreciation to their mothers and to acknowledge their indebtedness to them. The custom began when Miss Anne Jarvis, whose mother died in 1906, invited several friends to her home in Philadelphia on the first anniversary of her mother's death, to honor her memory. This was followed by a movement for the setting apart of a day for the remembrance of all mothers. In 1914, the Congress of the United States gave this day national sanction. It is a great idea.

A mother's shaping and nurturing role is paramount. A prime biblical example is that of the young man Timothy who was spiritually influenced by his mother and grandmother. The Apostle Paul said Timothy had *"a sincere faith, which first lived in his grandmother Lois and in his mother Eunice"* (2 Timothy 1:5). This resonates strongly with me. It was my mother who led me in a prayer of faith which resulted in Jesus Christ coming into my life to be my Savior and forever-friend when I was only ten years of age. Kneeling beside her bed that night so long ago I prayed the sinner's prayer. When I got up I knew Jesus had come to live inside of me and that my life was different. It has been so ever since. Thank you, Mom!

Nurturing young lives and nurturing faith is a tough job. One trade journal humorously noted: "Automation is a technological process that does all the work while you just sit there. When you were younger, this was called 'Mother.'"[16] At times mothers no doubt feel this is truly what is expected of them. Ruth Hampton described the job this way. "The most influential position in the nation today is held by a woman. She enforces law, practises medicine, and teaches – without degree, certificate of competence, or required training. She handles the nation's food, administers its drugs, and practises emergency first aid. This for all the spiritual, physical and mental ills of the American family. A man literally places his life and the lives of his children in the hands of this woman – his wife."[17] Mothering is no easy task. A little boy, who was told by his mother that it was God who made people good, responded, "Yes, I know it is God, but mothers help a lot."

Also powerful is the impact of grandmothers on young lives. They too are honored on Mother's Day. Sydney Martin noted that the value of Timothy's grandmother Lois' faith can be all the better appreciated in the light of a comment made by a missionary to India: "To make a sound Christian of a Hindu you have got to convert his grandmother."[18]

Pause to give thanks if you had such a mother and grandmother. If you didn't, here is your assignment: *"Fan into flame the gift of God which is in you ... for God did not give us a spirit of timidity, but a spirit of power, of love and of self-discipline"* (2 Timothy 1:6-7). This is your personal choice. Act on it. We can't blame problem parents for our own lack of faith. But we can thank God for mothers and grandmothers who positively influenced our faith. To them we say: "Happy Mother's Day!"

Mentoring – Pass it On!

To his mentee, Timothy, the early church leader, the Apostle Paul, urged *what you have heard from me in the presence of many witnesses entrust to faithful men who will be able to teach others also* (2 Timothy 2:2). What responsibility – and opportunity – do we, who have lived long, have to younger men and women who are coming after us? Let's put our minds and hearts into exploring that for a few minutes. Has it occurred to you that this may be one of the greatest gifts of older age – that we can powerfully influence younger people for good and for God?! In this verse, Paul is specifically pointing out the importance of passing on biblical teaching to younger leaders. However, there is also a broader sharing-life principle at work here.

Many (many) years ago when my wife and I were younger – a seminary couple in our twenties – we were embraced by the seniors in the church we attended for those four years of ministry preparation. I was, in fact, the teacher of the Berean (seniors) Bible class – a great honor for me. However, the far greater privilege was to be the recipient of the encouragement, care and love of these older adults as they shared their lives, resources and words with us. Many of them invited us into their homes, letting us gain a first-hand glimpse of their lives and families. As we got to know these folks one-on-one they told us their personal stories. It was so interesting! But more, their testimonies of God's faithfulness stimulated our own faith and imparted to us a sense that we too could be true to God well into our aged years. They gave us inspiration and hope.

As they met weekly in their Sunday School class we witnessed the good humor, the joy, the friendships, the openness to keep learning and the examples of service in their lives and in their exchanges with each other. This was what we too could look forward to in years ahead. Living was not just for the young. Imagine that! As "poor" seminary students (there was not a lot of extra money around in those formative years) who would not have been able to afford many "treats" in those days, these seniors often competed to be the first to invite us out for a scrumptious Sunday dinner at one of the city's famous buffet restaurants, or for coffee and pie after a Sunday evening service. We felt cherished and cared for and were many times encouraged by these expressions of love in the midst of frequent challenges that came in these years.

These good folks were a model for us. Imagine our joy as we witnessed the unfolding love story of an aged widow who moved to our church from another city. She met a godly aged widower and they fell deeply in love. Their wedding was the biggest event of that church year! To see the happiness that radiated from their lives in their marriage was a beautiful thing to behold. As newly marrieds ourselves, we were inspired by these newly married seniors!

Who do we now have in our lives that we can reach out to and pass on the faith? Recently one of our younger missionaries came back on home assignment. For a while, before he became a missionary, I had met with him over breakfast just to share my life and some of what I have learned. Now I feel a special affinity to him, due in part to the small role I played in mentoring him for a season. Dear friends, we can do this, both in specific acts of caring, as well as the inspiration of our lives. Let's invite some younger folks into our lives and share with them. Who knows the long-term impact it will have – both on them and on us?!

Let's Get Organized!

Organization. It's part of all our daily lives. In one of my favourite Charles Schultz "Peanuts" cartoons, Charlie Brown enters the TV room to watch a ball game, but finds Lucy already watching a romantic movie. The following exchange takes place:

Charlie Brown: "Lucy, change the channel."

Lucy (shaking her fist angrily): "No, I will not change the channel. Do you see these fingers? When they come together tightly they become a fist. This fist is almost a lethal weapon."

Charlie Brown (looking intently at his own fingers): "Why can't you guys ever get organized?"

"Let's get organized" we often hear said, and with good reason. Things go much better when well organized. Paul realized this was true of the Body of Christ and stated in Ephesians 4:16: *"From [Christ] the whole body, joined and held together by every supporting ligament, grows and builds itself up in love, as each part does its work."* Each of us has established organized patterns in how we live, from the sequence of how we start each day (shut off alarm, go to bathroom, brush teeth, put coffee on, get newspaper, etc.) to when and how we clean our house or pay our bills. When facing a new, seemingly overwhelming task, the first thing to do in making it manageable is to break it down into bite-sized chunks – the smaller tasks that make up the whole. Those tasks are then organized into the best sequence of events, and the people or resources needed to accomplish them, are all put in place. When approached in this way, the impossible begins to look possible and the big job gets done by completing a series of small jobs.

This applies to how we do ministry in our churches, and to how we set out to do ministry in the third third of our lives. As we analyze our ministries, sometimes we observe bottle necks that prevent growth or smooth functioning. Sometimes we see that the

27

way we've done things in the past is no longer working well for the present. In response, we may need to re-organize, to make some changes, or set some new goals, so things will work well again and, if in the church, the whole body will continue to be built up. If in our own lives, we'll fulfill the meaning and purpose we desire. A natural first-response to such changes is to resist. However, we each need to check that urge, take a look at how the changes might improve things, then embrace them for a better future for all. It's a good thing to organize for better effectiveness.

Legacy Leavers

A l-o-n-g time ago, when I was in elementary school, I wrote an article on Remembrance Day, commemorated on November 11 in Canada. My essay was selected as a winning entry and I received a trophy – my first and one of the few in my life. Even then, as a young boy, I had been touched by the legacy left to me by those who had laid down their lives for our country to preserve our freedoms. These many years later I am still moved by that legacy and stand silently with humble thanks at every cenotaph service I attend. The legacy left behind has the power to touch many lives for a long time.

Legacy. That descriptive refers to those who are in the season of life where they are finishing well and preparing to leave their legacy to following generations. However, leaving a legacy is not confined only to this generation. People of any age may leave a legacy. Many have. John F. Kennedy at age 46. Terry Fox at age 22. Winston Churchill at age 90. Jesus at age 33. You, me, at age ...?

In business and in church there are a small percentage of leaders at the top who are called "Level 5" Leaders (Jim Collins[19]), or "Acts 6/7" Leaders (Thom S. Rainer[20]). In essence, this 'less than 1% of all leaders,' are "Legacy Leaders". These leaders persevere to build something (a business, a ministry, a church, an influence) that will outlive themselves; something that will carry on to bless and help others long after they are gone from the scene. At great personal cost, they deal with the critics, keep focused on the long-term objectives, persevere and build to last. For them, the work is not about them, but about the mission all are called to. They accept slow progress, continually communicate love, are often reluctant leaders, remain humble and yet are strong leaders, focused on the future.

It is no small thing to live one's life with the constant objective of making the world better for those who will follow us. There is so much pressure to make life all about me. Yet Legacy Leaders step up out of that common crowd and decide that their lives will be greater than that. They live for what they will leave behind to bless others.

No one "just happens" to become a Legacy leader. There must be a choice – a clear decision, followed by a lifestyle of self-denial and servanthood. Hm-m-m. That reminds me of something someone else once said. *"If anyone would come after me, he must deny himself and take up his cross daily and follow me"* (Jesus, Luke 9:23). What legacy will we leave?

Productivity – Measuring My Years

Birthdays are interesting events; especially when of the milestone variety. They mark the annual passage of time. However, at a marker such as the one I recently passed (65!) they cause us to ask, 'where have so many years gone?' How quickly life passes. The Psalmist of the Bible warned us of this in Psalm 103:15: *"As for man, his days are like grass, he flourishes like a flower of the field; the wind blows over it and it is gone, and its place remembers it no more."* That doesn't seem possible when we are young. I feel like it was only yesterday that I was in my twenties. Then, before you know it, you've officially become a senior citizen 'with all the rights and privileges pertaining thereto!' Now it is time to reflect. What have I made of my life so far?

I read a great book by Tommy Barnett entitled, *The Power of a Half Hour*.[21] In it he expounded on how much good can be accomplished in half-hour blocks of time. Others' lives can be changed in the half hours we invest in them. He also warned that a half hour can destroy a life, based on the choices made in the face of overpowering temptation. Our lives today are a culmination of the half-hour investments of a life-time. If we invested well, living according to the biblical foundations of God's Word, we will be receiving results. However, if we lived in opposition to God's will and in disobedience to His commands, we will be getting consequences. Not only us. According to the Old Testament of the Bible, *"I, the Lord your God, am a jealous God, punishing the children for the sin of the parents to the third and fourth generation of those who hate me"* (Deuteronomy 5:9). In other words, some sins committed in rebellion against God will have lasting consequences in a family line that may impact children, grandchildren and even great grandchildren. God may forgive the sinner for his sin but the consequences cannot be stopped. How sobering. Some of us have lived long enough to have seen the truth of this played out, either in our own lives, or in the lives of our friends or acquaintances.

A more pleasant reality is that we can also make choices that have brought blessings on our family lines. I hope that is what we celebrate when we pass milestone birthdays. Do your children rise up and call you blessed? Or maybe the children of others whose lives you have positively touched in your lifetime? Again, the Psalmist says in 112:2, *"the generation of the upright will be blessed."* As a young pastor in my very first church the teens affectionately called me "PJ;" short for Pastor Johnston. I received a Facebook birthday greeting from one of those teens, now a man in his mid-forties. He said simply: "Happy birthday PJ. My favourite pastor." It warmed my heart. It also conveyed that perhaps a positive impact beyond my current knowing, was made on one life those many years ago.

Milestone birthdays are significant for reflection. But they are not end markers. The average lifespan for North Americans has increased dramatically. This means, Lord willing, we have many years left to invest half-hours in others that will impact them for eternity. Don't quit blessing. As long as we have life we have great work to do. *Do it heartily as to the Lord!* (Colossians 3:23, KJV). *"Do your best. Work from the heart for your real Master, for God, confident that you'll get paid in full when you come into your inheritance"* (*The Message*).

φ

Chapter 3

MISSION AND CALLING

Our Mission

A mission for baby boomers could we wrapped up in four words: CARING, SEEKING, REACHING and SERVING? This speaks to the purpose and ministry of those in the second half of life?! We are those who are called to CARE for all, to SEEK the Lord, to REACH those not-yet-in-the Kingdom and to SERVE as Servants of the Lord! This is the great mission we have together!

Our overarching purpose, in one word, is *"CARING."* We endeavor to care: *By Seeking the Lord, By Reaching the Lost* and *By Serving as Servants* of God. The Word of God, *The Bible*, gives us numerous admonitions to do all three. For example, *Seeking*: *"Seek the LORD while he may be found; call on him while he is near"* (Isaiah 55:6). *Reaching*: *"For the Son of Man came to seek and to save what was lost!"* (Luke 19:10). *Serving*: *"9But you are a chosen people, a royal priesthood, a holy nation, a people belonging to God, that you may declare the praises of him who called you out of darkness into his wonderful light. 10Once you were not a people, but now you are the people of God; once you had not received mercy, but now you have received mercy"* (1 Peter 2:9-10).

We have a great opportunity in working together, to touch each other's lives and the lives of those in our surrounding community who are not yet in the church, through these simple commitments to care by seeking the Lord, reaching the lost and serving all whom we can. The prayer for us is the prayer Jesus prayed for us in Matthew 9:36-37: *36When he saw the crowds, he had compassion* on them, because they were harassed and helpless, like sheep without a shepherd. *37Then he said to his disciples, "The harvest is plentiful but the workers are few. 38Ask the Lord of the harvest, therefore, to send out workers into his harvest field."* Will you join me on this mission?

Don't Wait: Do it Now!

Upon waking recently, I heard a wonderful sound: the singing of the birds. I was reminded of that verse in Song of Songs 2:12: *The flowers are springing up, and the time of singing birds has come, ...* (*New Living Translation*). Spring, a season of new beginnings, fresh starts and inner urges to get up and out and doing.

But, have you ever found yourself putting off really important things that you know you should do? You know, things like "... having friends over for ice cream or going on a picnic. Like using [your] fine china or celebrating a birthday . . . or slipping away for a weekend of relaxation and romance . . . or taking a cruise or traveling abroad . . . or sailing for a day. . . or spending a week away with the family.[22]

"Not this year ... but maybe, someday ..." you say. Reminds me of that mystical place that never comes ... "Someday Isle" [I'll]?!

Ann Wells wrote a thought-provoking article in the Los Angeles Times.

"My brother-in-law opened the bottom drawer of my sister's bureau and lifted out a tissue-wrapped package. . . . He discarded the tissue and handed me the slip. It was exquisite; silk, handmade and trimmed with a cobweb of lace. The price tag with an astronomical figure on it was still attached.

"'Jan bought this the first time we went to New York, at least eight or nine years ago. She never wore it. She was saving it for a special occasion. Well, I guess this is the occasion.'

"He took the slip from me and put it on the bed with the other clothes we were taking to the mortician. His hands lingered on the soft material for a moment, then he slammed the drawer shut and turned to me.

"'Don't ever save anything for a special occasion. Every day you are alive is a special occasion.'

35

"I remembered those words through the funeral and the days that followed when I helped him and my niece attend to all the sad chores that follow an unexpected death . . .

"I'm still thinking about his words, and they've changed my Life . . .

"I'm not 'saving' anything; we use our good china and crystal for every special event – such as losing a pound, getting the sink unstopped, the first camellia blossom . . .

"'Someday' and 'one of these days' are losing their grip on my vocabulary. If it's worth seeing or hearing or doing, I want to see and hear and do it now . . . I'm trying very hard not to put off, hold back, or save anything that would add laughter and luster to our lives."23

Every day is that special day you've been waiting for. Don't wait! The time for the singing of the birds has come. Spring, the season of new beginnings! What do you know you should do now? Don't wait. As for me, we've carved out three days at the end of this week to drive to Vernon to see our grandchildren! It's been a long time since Christmas. Life is short and time for being a Grandpa and Grandma to these three special little girls is fleeting.

Duty

A l-o-n-g time ago I was a Boy Scout. Well actually, before that, I was a Wolf Cub or Cub Scout. That was the junior organization of Scouting, the venerable institution launched by Lord Baden Powell of Gilwell based on his *Scouting for Boys* written in 1908. I hadn't thought much about the life-time impact those experiences made on me, but am now realizing the formative effect of those scouting values. One was that of duty. The Scout Promise, repeated at every pack or troop meeting, went: "I promise that I will do my best, To do my **duty** to God and the Queen" (I'm Canadian, remember), "To help other people at all times, And to carry out the spirit of the Scout Law." The Scout motto, "Be prepared," meant always being prepared, among other things, to do our duty.

Duty. Something about Septembers (return to school after summer break, or to work after summer vacation) is synonymous with duty. Ugh! Yet, necessary. Duty is a moral commitment or obligation that should result in action. It means fulfilling our commitments – to work, to family, to country, to the organizations with whom we have chosen to partner. There is that in us which prefers freedom – from responsibility, from commitments, from being 'tied down.' Yet that exists more in the realm of fantasy than real life. Those who follow that calling become irresponsible freeloaders and a burden to society. But it is the dutiful who bring stability and dependability to life. It's a tougher calling, true, yet absolutely necessary. If I have an accident, face a medical emergency, or if my house catches fire, I want to know that the policeman, paramedic and fireman are standing by, ready to do their duty at a moment's notice.

Are you chafing internally at returning to your duties this next season (if indeed you were fortunate to have a summer or other break from them, even if only briefly)? Fret not. We need you. You are the glue that holds together all that is worthwhile. Winston Churchill is quoted as saying: "All the great things are simple, and many can be expressed in a single word: freedom, justice, honor, duty, mercy, hope." Duty is a great thing. Never underestimate its importance.

There are critics of duty. They claim it stifles creativity and free expression; that it turns us into mindless automatons. Conversely, it was E. Stanley Jones who declared: "The disciplined will rule the world."[24] The greatest contributions to society, the greatest creativity and positive impact, the most heroic actions, arise out of the dutiful, disciplined persons who faithfully serve at their posts, fulfilling their daily responsibilities.

As we return to our duties and commitments to work, to families, to church, to our organizations after a break away, put on a happy face. Sing a song in your heart. Yes, this is duty, but it is also great joy. We will make a difference in the lives of others. That is more than duty. That is privilege! Be prepared to do your duty. Oh, and one more thing. The Scout Slogan: "Do a good turn daily." We can do that while fulfilling our duties! Who knows what joy we will bring?!

Humidity, Hay and Hard Work

Haying season. The summer month of July brings back to me memories of haying on the southern Ontario farm where I grew up. Hot weather, high humidity, back breaking work, profuse sweat and long workdays were synonymous with this month. My Dad and his three healthy sons worked side-by-side to bring in thousands of square bales of hay each summer. First came the mowing, sometimes the tedding (a machine that threw the hay into the air to help it better dry), raking the hay into windrows and then the actual baling. Sometimes the bales were left where they dropped out of the baler. Other times one of us stood on the stooker behind the baler, stooking the bales into pyramid shaped stacks which would better withstand any rain that might fall before they could be taken into the barn. A pull on a lever dropped the stook on the ground and another one was started as the next bale came out. Oh yes, the man operating the stooker had to be sure not to drop the stook on a sidewise incline or on top of a ground-hog hole's mound, or the whole stook might fall over. Then the baling operation had to stop while the stook was rebuilt a second time. Extra work. Ugh!

Once baled, it was time to bring the hay in. Grabbing the strings of each 50+ pound bale with both hands we would swing it high into the air towards the top of the wagon load. The man on top would grab the bales coming at him from both sides and build the load until no more could be added. The man on the tractor had the easiest job as he maneuvered the wagon between bales, then headed towards the barn with the loaded wagon. Once there, the bales were placed onto a moving elevator ramp that took them high up into a door near the roof of the barn. At the end of their journey they fell off the elevator onto the mow. Two or three of us worked in that dusty, enclosed, hot place grabbing the bales with bale hooks and dragging them across the mow to be placed in layers. There they stayed until the time came for them to be fed to the livestock in the cold days of winter.

This back breaking work built stamina, strength and muscular physiques – of which, as young teens, we were rightfully proud. We learned to endure discomfort, itchy uncomfortableness, heat, dust and sweat as the price of diligent effort. The work ethic learned has stood us all in good stead throughout our lifetimes. But one other major lesson came out of this experience for me: I learned that I did not want to grow up to be a farmer! July should instead be a month for vacations, preferably camping by a lake in a climate that is not nearly as humid! More Julys have since been spent doing that than were expended in haying on the farm in my youth.

None of us looked forward to the hard work of this season. But the thing about haying was that at a set time of the year it must be done. No delays were permissible because of distractions, not feeling like it, or other excuses. Growth seasons, weather and temperatures all determined when the job was required. To procrastinate could mean losing the crop and having no feed for our livestock the rest of the year. That would mean disaster. Life is like that – for all of us. What tough thing are you needing to do "right now?" Get at it. Don't delay. Get it done. Do the tough work required. Oh yes. There was always a feeling of great satisfaction when haying was done and the barns were filled with carefully-built mows. Work now, but look forward to the pay-off.

Revised Perspective

The new year is typically a time for thinking back, reviewing your past and making plans and resolutions for the year ahead. The backward look can prove painful. Many life experiences are so tough to go through, that we wonder to ourselves why God would ever allow them and of what possible good they could ever be. The memory can leave a bitter taste.

One winter while in college 1,300 miles from home, I managed to make my way back to the family farm for Christmas. Yes, it was a white Christmas; white from a couple feet of snow on the ground and bitter cold as well. I headed home, anticipating family times gathered in the warmth from the two stoves in the farmhouse, lots of time for rest and the making of pleasant memories far from the rigours of college studies and interminable assignments. That was my anticipation. The reality was altogether different.

Shortly after arrival, the pump in the well burned out. No water was available for house usage and the farm animals had to be driven over a mile each day to drink water from a stream – after gaining access by breaking a hole in the ice. And, the pump had to be replaced. It was located about 15 feet below ground level inside a four-foot diameter concrete tile well.

My memories from that Christmas are of long hours of hard labor alongside my Dad, working either in a freezing cold confined space or in the exposed outside air, removing the old pump, finding a new one to replace it, and then trying to position the new pump to be installed without dropping the 90 feet of casing that accessed water far below. Interspersed with this energy draining job were the regular farm chores, plus over three hours each day spent driving the cattle to be watered and home again. Icy cold, back-breaking labour and long days summarized my memories of that experience. Why did this have to happen? Farm life was hard enough at best without such a mishap in the depth of winter. With limited time for a vacation with family, why was most of it consumed with this setback? Why indeed.

In my reflection on this recalled memory, I gained a new insight. On the upside, hours were spent working alongside my dear father who was then a little younger than I am now. He would have turned 100 this year. However, he has already been gone for eleven years. That experience, so dreadful at the time, in hindsight is precious because of the time spent with my Dad. Yes, it was laborious, but in working as a team we got the job done. The well worked once more and water was available for both people and animals. The discomfort of the work is long gone. The happiness of the memory remains.

Are you facing some unbearable hardships right now? Are you protesting, "Why me?! Why now?!" Stop. Breathe deeply. Relax. Allow for a revised perspective. Your present ordeal, with time, may one day become a precious memory. Look around and ask instead, "I wonder what God is up to in this? What is it I need to be taking note of and even enjoying?" Thanks, dear God.

India Contrasts

After I returned from a mission trip to India, "What was it like?" was the oft-asked question. Best answer? It is a land of contrasts: wealth alongside poverty; religiosity alongside commercialism; hustle and bustle alongside peace and introspection; and magnificent architecture alongside trash and debris. Opposites were everywhere. Over 9 million people live in Bangalore, the third largest city of India, which is among the top ten preferred entrepreneurial locations in the world.

In reflecting on my one-week visit I observed other contrasts: those between this so-called developing world country and our own (self-perceived) advanced and civilized North American nations. A plethora of personal temples on home properties exalting the Hindu monkey, elephant or other gods is in contrast to the high-end car models and luxury homes testifying to our North American gods of mammon. An abundance of local Indian eateries and street food vendors were found alongside the familiar KFC, Baskin-Robbins, McDonalds, Pizza Hut, Subway, Taco Bell, Quizno Subs and other fast food outlets. Sidewalk "factory outlet" vendors selling shoes, t-shirts and other clothing items were found in proximity to stores and offices bearing labels such as Levi, Bata, Puma, Reebok, Hush Puppies, Ricoh, Samsung, Ericsson, Nokia, KPMG, ING, Accenture, Curves, HerbaLife and Louis Vuitton! In a penthouse suite atop the largest, most modern high-rise mall in the city, lived one of the country's wealthiest billionaires who owns it all.

Religion was another realm of contrasts. In this nation of Hindu, Sikh, Buddhist and Krishna Consciousness temples, one observed signs including: "Jesus Only," "I love Jesus," "Have Faith in God," and Hope Chapel – "Challenge the Impossible with Christ." Church and other buildings included: Immaculate Convent, Campus Crusade for Christ, Little Sisters of Jesus, Praise Jesus Church, Baldwin Methodist College, Mother Theresa's Missionaries of Charity, Church of Christ, South India Assemblies of God, St. Mark's Cathedral, Kingdom Hall of Jehovah's Witnesses and the Bangalore YMCA. I had to remind myself that I was in India, not Vancouver. "Astrology – Computer horoscopes here" was a sign that would have been just as at home in North America!

In North America, which has seen the removal of the 10 commandments from courthouses and the Lord's Prayer from schools, I found irony in the large slogan engraved in the façade of the India Karnataka State Government building: "Government Work is God's Work." I toured the Church of South India Hospital whose byline was: "Compassion and Caring for Over a 100 Years." Coming from a nation which has diligently removed most evidence of religious affiliation from its hospitals, even the Grace Hospitals founded and run for decades by the Salvation Army, I was struck by the prayer request box located at the reception desk and scripture verses on the walls such as Jeremiah 33:6 – *"Behold I will bring to you health and healing and I will heal you and will reveal to you an abundance of peace and truth."*

Holy cows are given free reign to wander the streets forging for food, while here dogs are required to be on a leash in all places except dog parks. Beautiful century-old stone built churches, with stained glass windows and steeples reaching to the skies are to be found in both India and Vancouver. Wall to wall traffic filling every empty space, drivers riding on each other's bumpers, only slowing, not-stopping for cross-traffic, so close to each other that it is dangerous to put your arm out the window, were a North American driver's nightmare. Yet, there were no collisions and the traffic of millions of vehicles flowed seamlessly. Note this bumper sticker wisdom: "You only live once but if you do it right once is enough."

So, which is the better country? Which the more Christian, I mused? The jury is still out.

φ

Chapter 4

AGING AND INFLUENCE

Positive Aging

When I was a child at school we played the game, "Hide and Seek." The person who was "it" counted to 100, then loudly announced, "Ready or not, here I come," and ran out to catch as many people as he or she could. As we age into the senior years we will face many changes. "Ready or not, here they come!" How we face them will make a world of difference to the people who surround us. We can rebelliously fight every change, resisting with all we are worth, negatively complaining about each upset thrust upon us, or we can positively anticipate them and make life as pleasant as possible for all around! A well-known pastor made this comment about change: "Don't fear change. Welcome it as an opportunity! If change is a great problem, it is also a grand human hope. ... Thank God we are not created to be rigid, non-changing objects of marble, granite or steel!"[25]

The matter of housing and care is a major area of change many seniors must face. Declining health or decreasing capacities may necessitate a move from the traditional family home into some other type of housing or care facility. There is no other word for it: this kind of change is <u>hard</u>. But it may also be inevitable. Will you have to face that in the year ahead? Maybe? Let me encourage you to decide right now that you will set your attitude to a positive setting. You will say: "I accept that this is coming and will embrace it, make the most of it, trust that God will be with me in it and that good will come out of this both for me and those who lovingly care for me." If you will choose now (and only you can make that choice) to approach this change in this way it will be a huge relief to those who have responsibility for you. This may include your adult children as well as the caregivers who will work with you in your new home environment.

As a pastor, son and nephew working with senior adults I've observed both scenarios. After my Dad's death, my Mom could no longer continue on her own in her condo and needed to move to a lovely assisted-living facility. She resisted, rebelled and made life difficult for many – especially my younger sister who lived nearby in that community far from where I lived. But it did not stop with family. She made life difficult for her caregivers. One night in a fit of indignation, because no one would respond to her call to come and warm her bean bag to place on an aching muscle, she reached for her phone and dialled 9-1-1! Fire department emergency personnel, facility staff and family members were all stressed by this one act. Looking back, it's kind of humorous now, but it wasn't then. The rest of Mom's story turned out better and demonstrated the opposite scenario. She was later moved to the nursing home area of this facility. By then she had accepted that this was a good place for her to be and had changed her attitude. Her last years there were much more positive and enjoyable for her and all those around her.

Yes, these kinds of changes are hard. But we can make them so much better for ourselves and those we love through proactive choices and positive attitudes. Furthermore, God promises to give us His grace so we will evidence His nature as we embrace our future.

Teen Lessons for Aging

The onset of the cooler wet weather of fall makes it apparent that my kayaking season will soon be over. Reflection on the past summer's on-the-water experiences jogged distant memories of canoeing adventures in my teen years.

I was privileged to attend a wilderness Scout camp in my mid-teens. We were taught proper paddling techniques and canoe management. Each summer our learning culminated in a three day, 50-mile-long canoe trip that tested our mettle. We learned to stay relatively dry – not warm – but dry, sleeping under our canoes in heavy rainfall. Slogging through mud up to our knees while carrying heavy backpacks and canoes over a one-mile-long portage, was the low point of those journeys. We wondered if we would make it! Some collapsed and had to be encouraged by our leaders – not always gently – to load up and try again. A few left either their backpack or canoe behind, made the journey with one item, then trudged all the way back to get the other item, thus navigating the muddy portage not once, but three times, in order to get everything through. In those moments, I was thankful for the heavy work of farm life that had built up my strength and stamina. Those low portage moments were offset by the sheer pleasure of paddling across calm, beautiful lakes in God's great outdoors. As we paddled, we sang out our favorite mantra: "Lily pad roots are like candy to the moose!" Crazy, eh?! Occasionally we would catch a glimpse of a majestic moose.

This proved to be good preparation. A few years later as a nineteen-year-old, I was to lead a dozen youth offenders on three-day canoe trips on the Lake of the Woods in northwestern Ontario, as part of their two-week camping experiences at a Youth for Christ camp. Many of these young men had never been outside of a city in their lives. This was a totally foreign experience to them. With minimal instruction in canoeing, we pushed their limits and tested their mettle. Once underway, there was no turning back, for the canoe was our only transportation to get back to camp. There were humorous moments, such as the day we flipped our canoe on perfectly flat, calm water! Thank you to a portly bowman leaning way over, digging his paddle in really deep to scoop water at those in another canoe in the midst of a vigorous water fight! His strategy backfired. Instead of splashing water, he rolled our canoe and we were the ones who ended up getting soaked.

The scariest moment for me as the leader, came as we crossed a large body of water in a building storm, paddling through frighteningly high waves. We were far short of that day's destination, but I made a decision to head for land and pitch camp in the first location we could reach, rather than risk carrying on in such dangerous weather. We survived the night and eventually made it safely home.

Where am I going with these stories? As many of us negotiate the new frontier of aging, much is unknown and there are unexpected dangers along the way. Are we not often tempted to fear?! Stop. Reflect. Remember the skills you have learned and the experiences of earlier life. Recall how many times, with God's help, you made it safely through great challenges. Draw on that assurance. God will not abandon you now. You will negotiate these years successfully. What's more, you'll build your repertoire of stories to share with others. Why, it will be as easy as ... paddling a canoe! Enjoy the journey.

Aging: It's Time.

In a youth-oriented culture such as ours, aging has often been seen as a negative: something to be avoided at best or dreaded at worst. How deprived we have been to view it in this manner. Slowly we are maturing in our understanding of this unavoidable and yes, to be favorably anticipated, stage of life.

I returned from the city of Regina where I preached at my wife's aunt's funeral. She passed away in the ninety-eighth year of a very full life. She had remained extremely active up to her last three or four years. Then, following a series of small heart attacks, she began to slow down. In this season, she wondered why she was still here and why God had not taken her home to heaven. Why did she linger when she could no longer do all the charitable work and compassionate deeds she had thrived upon prior to this? Why indeed? Why do any of us linger or need to go through a stage of often diminished strength, energy or even ability? What good could there possibly be in this? Those are fair questions.

While pondering this dilemma in preparation for my aunt's message I discovered a wonderful perspective in the writings of Pastor Max Lucado. Max wrote in *Traveling Light*: "Aging is God's idea. ... It's one of the ways he keeps us headed homeward. We can't change the process, but we can change our attitude. ... What if we looked at the aging body as we look at the growth of a tulip? Do you ever see ... gardeners weep as the bulb begins to weaken? Of course not. ... Tulip lovers rejoice the minute the bulb weakens. 'Watch that one,' they say. 'It's about to blossom.'

"Could it be heaven does the same? The angels point to our bodies. The more frail we become, the more excited they become. 'Watch that lady in the hospital, they say. 'She's about to blossom.' 'Keep an eye on the fellow with the bad heart. He'll be coming home soon.'"[26] This earth was not her final home. Nor is it ours. As our bodies weaken and our strength diminishes it is natural to start longing for our real home – our eternal one. God can use this season to ready us to be with him ... forever!

Don't fear aging. Choose an attitude that will enable you to see in it God's purposes fulfilled. C. S. Lewis had the right perspective. He wrote "How Old Are You?" in *A Grief Observed*:

> *"Age is a quality of mind:*
>
> *If you have left your dream behind,*
>
> *If hope is cold*
>
> *If you no longer look ahead,*
>
> *If your ambition fires are dead—*
>
> *Then you are old.*
>
> *But if from life you take the best,*
>
> *And if in life you keep the jest,*
>
> *If love you hold;*
>
> *No matter how the years go by,*
>
> *No matter how the birthdays fly,*
>
> *You are not old."*[27]

With a brave face on, choose the positive approach and live to see God's plan fulfilled in your aging life chapter.

Connecting: Impacting

One month the last church I served in hosted a memorial service for a lady whose life was touched by seniors' ministries. Enduring a life-time struggle with mental illness she was one of society's socially awkward members. We, and they, never quite know how to act in each other's presence. Avoidance might be easier, yet God's love compels us to engage. But is it worth the effort, we may ask ourselves? I want to encourage you that, Yes, it is!

In this dear lady's case, her daughters testified that their sweet Mom always wanted to be a good mother, but was unable to deliver on that desire. A loving grandmother stepped in and made up much of the difference for them in their growing up years. In that era of life, the church connected with them as children and laid caring relational foundations. Now as adults, with a desire to honor their Mom, they returned to the church they knew had loved them in the past. In their Mom's infrequent contacts with the church, caring people had made the effort and connected with her, strengthening that bond of caring. That month we had opportunity to deepen the relationship with that family once more by conducting the memorial service. Connecting. Opportunities are all around us. Impacting – in ways we may hardly realize.

One Sunday each month were designated as "Family of God" Sundays at this church, and we often heard testimonies of children and teens who were instrumental in bringing parents to a saving relationship with Jesus Christ. In my lifetime, I have met grandparents who likewise reached across generations and were used by God to bring grandchildren – and others – to faith in Christ. May I make an encouraging appeal to all of us in the second half of our life and ministry? None of us are too old (or young) to make the effort to reach out to connect with others. All that is required is to briefly remove our self-focus, put on an others-focus and then to reach out to those God puts in our path whom we can touch in Jesus' name. Whatever issues others may have, our call is to share the love of Jesus by caring. We never know where that story will end. Maybe it will be in another memorial service a few years down the road in which links to a relationship with Jesus Christ will be further strengthened. Let's engage in connecting. Who knows what the impact may be?!

Needed: Kindness.

What kind of face do you have? Facial treatments and skin care products are today a multi-million (billion?!) dollar business. But that's not the field I want to talk about. Rather, what do people see when they look at your face ... and behaviors?

"A tiny girl waited at a street crossing until Lord Shaftesbury came along. Then she asked, 'Please, sir, will you help me across the road?' Safely on the other side, she thanked the unknown gentleman, who playfully asked why she had chosen him as her escort. 'Because, sir, you looked so kind.'"[28]

Does my countenance have that effect on people? Does yours? Or, do the storm-clouds on our faces tend rather to scare people away?! *"Be ye kind one to another, tenderhearted, forgiving each other, even as God also in Christ forgave you"* it says in the Bible (Ephesians 4:32).

"How do we go about doing that?" you may ask. Probably, in a hundred different ways. Here's one: The simplest way to be kind to people is to be nice to them. Kindness and thoughtfulness are interlocked with genuine courtesy – almost a lost art in the modern world. A lady boarded an overcrowded bus. Immediately a man stood to give her a seat. She was so taken by surprise that she fainted. When she revived, she turned to the man and said, "Thank you." Then he fainted.

"Courtesy costs us nothing except the discipline required to develop it. But it pays off in the priceless returns of goodwill, happiness, and enrichment."[29]

Kindness requires day-by-day, moment-by-moment sacrifice – sacrificing my priorities and self-centredness for the priorities and welfare of others. This really isn't much of a sacrifice, for it pays such outstanding benefits. Do not underestimate the warmth that floods our beings when we have gone out of our way to assist someone else, then received in return their broad, warm smile and simple words of thanks. Knowing you have lifted someone's burden and made their day a little better because of an unselfish act done on their behalf is rewarding, even if they are not aware of it at the moment. But, you know!

"Therefore, as we have opportunity, let us do good to all people, especially to those who belong to the family of believers" (Galatians 6:10). If you are a Christian believer, kindness must start with fellow Christians. Do not take them for granted or be unkind to them. There is a tendency to do this and so the Word underlines a warning not to neglect, but to be sure to treat each other well! Do good: be kind!

I hope you are having a great day. If not, smile at someone and make their day great for them!! It will probably turn your day around as well.

What is Truth?

"You must always tell the truth." It was a lesson drilled into me by my parents while growing up. It seems obvious. Yet, we live in a day filled with lying. Jesus faced this issue. When brought before Pilate in his final week on earth, before being sentenced to death based on a pack of lies brought by false witnesses, the two of them had this conversation.

"Are you the king of the Jews, Jesus? Who are you anyway?" Pilate asked him. Jesus answered, "You are right in saying I am a king. In fact, for this reason I was born, and for this I came into the world, to testify to the truth. Everyone on the side of truth listens to me."

"What is truth?" Pilate asked. (John 18:37-38). "Who am I to believe?" Jesus said he had come into the world to testify to the truth. The falsely lying Jewish leaders said they were telling the truth. Little wonder Pilate threw up his hands in exasperation.

Earlier in John 14:6 Jesus had declared: *"I am the way and the truth and the life. No one comes to the Father except through me."* That's a definitive declaration of his divinity. It underlined the finality of His Word! The truth! The way! The life!

Things are not much changed today. We live in a time when so-called Christians can hold some amazing views of what they think "truth" really is. The clear Word of God can become so twisted in thinking, that believers defend evil and criticize God's good.

A Barna poll a few years ago exposed this reality. It revealed not only that two-thirds of American people believed there was no such thing as absolute truth, but worse, that "53 percent of those claiming to be Bible-believing, conservative Christians said there is no such thing as absolute truth. A majority of those who follow the One who says, 'I am the truth,' profess not to believe in truth. ... Although 70 percent of all Americans believe it is important to do what the Bible teaches, two-thirds of this same group reject moral absolutes. Schizophrenic."[30]

Brothers and sisters, we must be clear on the lifestyle God's Word calls us to live. The Bible describes it well. When confronted with those who would call evil good and good evil, we cannot give in so as to appear friendly and non-judgmental. Jesus was clear: "Everyone on the side of truth listens to me." Implication? Those who will not listen to me are not on the side of truth! That's not a group I want to be found numbered among when my accounting before God comes. Know God's truth – and evaluate all you see, do and hear in light of that – not by a subjective feeling of what you would like the truth to be.

Chapter 5

YOUR STORY, YOUR LEGACY

Tell Your Story

While in my teens my maternal grandfather suffered a stroke that robbed him of short-term memory. He came to live with us for over two years until his death. Daily we endured repetitious questions: "What day is it?" "What am I doing here?" Patiently we would answer. In addition, he told us familiar stories from his past, favourite sayings, favourite jokes. To this day, I remember many of them. For example: "You can fool some of the people some of the time, and even all of the people some of the time; but you can't fool all of the people all of the time!" It was hard to forget these when they were so oft-told! Over time his sayings and his stories became my own.

My father was a quiet, rather shy man. That is, until you got him going on the stories of his past, of our farm neighbours and of our extended family. He knew who was related to who and could explain what "a cousin, twice-removed" meant! Dad could go non-stop for hours at a time if we provided him an audience. As a consequence, we had a sense of where we came from, who this family was that we belonged to, what kind of neighbourhood we had grown up in and the history of the neighbours who made up this community. The great need for "uncommon common sense" was one of his favourite maxims. Dad's stories gave us context, history and a sense of belonging. I don't think we ever said, "Oh Dad! You've already told us that story." We loved to hear them again and again.

It's a funny thing about my Dad's and my Grandpa's stories, jokes and sayings. The oddest things now will trigger memories of them. In my moment of remembering, it is as if they were present and I can hear them telling it all over again. Although they are now in heaven it's as if they once more come alive for me. Beyond the memory, is the point of the story or saying: a moral, a character guideline, or an historical context from my past. It influences me here and now. Where did that phrase come from, "who being dead, yet speaketh?"[31] Yes, they do.

Which leads me to ask: are we telling our stories – especially those of us who tend to be shy or reserved? Will our children and grandchildren have an historical context that will give them family identity from previous generations? Will they know of family heroes who modeled for them hard work, faithfulness, perseverance, caring or integrity? We all need such role models and what an impact if they come from our own family lines! What about our spiritual heritage? Do they know how God first started working in our lives or perhaps even in previous generations? Are we giving them a sense of belonging to the branch of God's family with our last names? Have we so thrilled them with the story of our conversion that they long to know and follow our same Jesus? What a great opportunity we have before us through simply telling our stories. Say, did I tell you about the time that ...?

[To prime your pump in getting started, go online to: www.your-life-your-story.com].

Share Your Story

"I grew up on a small mixed farm in southern Ontario. Sunday church attendance was part of my upbringing. My parents were hard-working, good people. Then, in her mid-life, my mother went through a life-changing conversion experience. Jesus Christ came alive to her when she trusted in Him alone as her Savior. She soon shared that experience with me and everyone else who would listen. Although a relatively good little boy, I became aware of my own sinful condition and of the bad things I had already done. One evening I knelt by my mother's bed in prayer, confessed to God that I knew my sin separated me from Him, and in child-like faith, prayed to invite Jesus Christ to come into my heart, forgive me of my sins and to give me His free gift of eternal life. He came! In that moment, at ten years of age, I knew God's forgiveness and that He had come to live in me. It's now over fifty-six years later and He has never left.

"Through the many challenges of my life, the peace and presence of God has remained at the center. He has enabled me to overcome every setback and has guided my every step – in finding the wonderful woman I married, in all my education, in calling me to become a Christian pastor, in the places where I have served and in the family we raised. I've experienced the joy of knowing God's presence with me every day of my life. I have the deep assurance that when my journey here on earth ends, I will be with Him eternally in the home in heaven He has prepared for me. Experiencing God's love made a life-long difference in me."

That – in two paragraphs and 90 seconds of speaking – is the testimony of my life with God. It doesn't begin to tell the whole story. That would take volumes of books. But in the minute and a half of attention you might be willing to give me in a casual conversation, you've heard how I became aware of my need for God's salvation, how I experienced it through faith-filled confession and prayer, and of the life-long impact God's daily presence has made in my sixty-six plus years of living. If you did not personally know God, might this 90-second story start you to thinking about the deep unmet need in your life and start you to wondering if maybe something like this is what you've been looking for, even longing for, all of your life? Could it launch you on a journey toward your own conversion and eternal destiny to be with God forever? Possibly it could.

That, my believing Christian friends, is why we need to have ready a simple, brief testimony that we can share in the midst of a casual conversation with anyone God brings across our path. *"Always be prepared to give an answer to everyone who asks you to give the reason for the hope that you have. But do this with gentleness and respect"* (1 Peter 3:15). Gently, respectfully, we sow the seed. God will give the increase. The Holy Spirit takes our simple testimonies, energizes them in the minds and hearts of those we share with, convicts them of the truth of sin and righteousness, and uses that to bring them to himself in salvation.

Are you ready to share your story? Why not get a pen and piece of paper right now and write out your own brief testimony of how you came to know God and what He has done in your life? Refine it. Time it. Shorten it to the basics. Memorize it. Be ready to tell it. Only God knows the impact your story will have in the life of someone who is longing to know Him as you do.

All the Saints

In the church calendar, November 1st is All Saints Day, following hard on Reformation Sunday, commemorated on the fourth Sunday of October. On that day, we recall the huge debt the church owes to a saint named Martin Luther, who in courage and boldness launched what became known as the Protestant Reformation. The first day of November was set by Pope Gregory III in the early eighth century as "All Saints Day," a day to remember John the Baptist and all those who had been martyred for their faith in Christ. Pope Gregory IV in the ninth century extended this day, also known as "All Hallows' Day," to the entire church. The vigil leading up to this feast day was popularly called "Hallowe'en", "Halloween" or "All Hallows' Eve". William H. How (1823-1897) wrote an often-sung hymn that went, in part:

> "1. For all the saints, who from their labors rest,
>
> Who Thee by faith before the world confessed,
>
> Thy Name, O Jesus, be forever blessed.
>
> Alleluia, Alleluia!
>
> 2. Thou wast their Rock, their Fortress and their Might;
>
> Thou, Lord, their Captain in the well fought fight;
>
> Thou, in the darkness drear, their one true Light.
>
> Alleluia, Alleluia!"

Luther was one such saint in the sixteenth century. There are many more.

Approaching this month and ruminating on this day, I recalled how the apostle Paul often addressed his letters, "To the saints at ..." such and such a city. These were then-living believers who had not been killed for their commitment to following Christ Jesus. Early in my life I learned that in a sense, all of us are "saints." Paul's use of the term did not imply perfection or "super" status. It simply named all who are in Christ, saints. In that sense, you and I – if we have trusted in Christ alone as our Savior – are indeed, saints! We are. Common, ordinary everyday people doing what we each can to faithfully serve our Lord. One missionary referred to those who had prayed for him while on the mission field as "Saints Anonymous!" "The unseen, unsung deeds of people with small roles in the Kingdom must never be underestimated," he said.

Continuing to meditate on this theme I was next reminded of some of the saints in my life who made a profound impact on me in my early years. One was a grade 4 Sunday School teacher, Mrs. Dorothy Best, who taught us in a corner classroom off the church platform in a little town church of 40 to 50 people. When I visited her a few years ago, then a woman in her early-80's, she downplayed the role she felt she had in my life. Nevertheless, she made an impact on me for having committed to teaching our little class. Another was one of my early pastors, Rev. Leonard E. Sparks, formerly a Salvation Army missionary to India, then pastoring that same little church. One Sunday was mission's night and he had asked if he could dress me in an Indian costume as part of his object lesson. Somehow with farm chores and the long drive in from the country, our family arrived late to the service. But, he had waited for us, quickly put the east-Indian attire on me and included me in that service. In that and a number of other small ways this caring pastor profoundly influenced me, I believe, towards a lifetime in Christian ministry. These were some of my saints.

There were other saints, as well. In my first year away from home at college, I attended a small church of probably 40-70 in attendance. The pastor, Rev. Owen Underwood, was a dear man of God. We arrived in town unannounced, my mother and I, and showed up at his door. He helped me find room and board with a great family from the church and my Mom was able to leave me in good care when she returned home. Pastor Underwood, a quiet, gentle man, faithfully cared for his flock (which now included me), led joyful worship services each Sunday, preached solid messages, directed a youth choir of which I became a part and facilitated a youth/young adult group who embraced me as one of their own.

This saint of God and his dear wife and family helped make that a memorable, and good year for me.

From there I moved to another large city where I lived during my four years at Bible college. There were so many saints there who impacted my life. One was Mae Harper. This dear aboriginal woman was the head cook in our college dining room. We ate our meals family style. For a year, I worked closely with her as the head waiter, directing the serving staff who brought the food to each table, cleared away the dishes and served their fellow students. The food she prepared was always delicious, something we all appreciated. But far greater was the impact of this dear, friendly woman who became a surrogate mother to many young college students, lonely in their first experiences away from home. How we loved "Ma" Harper! She is still living, now in her 80's, in a care home in that same city. She is lovingly cared for by her adult children and still beloved by so many of us who are now scattered around the world.

Moving on to my seminary years, one saint who had a profound impact on my life was my pastor, Rev. Dick Young. I have often said that I learned as much from my experience in that church under his mentorship as I did from my four years in seminary working on my two Masters degrees! Lately I have reminisced on the lesson I learned from him about relationships – that the heart of a healthy church is the level of healthy relationships that exist within it. That is what made that experience so formative and the quality and example of relationship flowed out of the life and care of this dear pastor. I've since served in churches that lacked this essential dynamic and the comparison is dramatic. This pastor preached warm, yet challenging messages, loved on people as friends, visited those who were in hospital, was a strong administrator and directed seminary students in our field education experiences within and without the church. We learned much from him. At the same time, we sensed how much he loved each one of us. Another great saint!

It has been almost 30 years since we left the first church we pastored for nine years. Recently we returned to that city for a visit and worshiped at this church. The current pastor is another great saint. She and her then newly married husband were young people just getting started in ministry in that area when we left. Later, her first husband died tragically and suddenly, leaving her as a young Mom of two children. Subsequently she met and married a fine businessman who supported her in her work. Rose Brower-Young became the pastor of this church I loved and had once pastored. She is doing a fabulous job and building into the lives of the many whom she loves on and ministers to week after week. To me, she is an inspiration as another of God's dear saints.

Who are the saints who have blessed and influenced your life? As we think of "All Saints Day" why not take a few minutes to recall and to give thanks to God for them. Perhaps we could even contact them and express that thanks personally. Further, to who are you being an inspiring saint? We may never know the full impact we have on others but be sure, if we are allowing God to work in and through us, then we are touching others. Be faithful, dear saints. This then, is my tribute to "all the saints" – both dead and living all around us right now.

φ

Chapter 6

God's Guidance & Timing

God Whispers and Guidance

"What does God want me to do with my life?" We start asking that question early in life, and it often recurs as life progresses – certainly as we enter the third third of life. Has this question (or one similar) crossed your mind lately? And how in the world do we discover God's will for us anyway?

E. Stanley Jones observed: "Many Christians know little or nothing about personal guidance from God. They go from event to event and live a kind of hand-to-mouth spiritual existence – a spiritual and moral opportunism. They have no sense of working out a plan of life under God's guidance. They have little or no sense of destiny, of mission. ... Hence, they have little sense of accountability to God and little sense of His guidance in their lives. Hence their impact upon life is feeble. Only people who have a sense of mission and who are under God's guidance accomplish things."[32]

Wow. If true, then we had better discover how to know God's will so our lives will have impact for God. As I've perused a number of authors on this matter I've discovered a common denominator. Knowing God's will requires stilling ourselves before Him ... and listening for Him to speak ... through His Word (the Bible) that He will bring alive for us ... and through the quiet inner voice of His Holy Spirit whispering to us. We must train our ears to hear and understand His voice. Jesus said, *"my sheep hear my voice and they follow me"* (John 10:27).

Christian psychiatrist, Dr. John White, tells us how. "Take time. Don't hurry. Spread the matter out before the Lord. Keep a Bible handy as you pray, though not with the idea of receiving guidance like a horoscope reading. Rather it can help you recall godly principles you have forgotten or have been neglecting. Find the passages where the principles are explained. Write down how they specifically apply to your circumstances. As you do you will notice that the tumult in your heart is lessening. Something of God's quietness will bring a measure of peace. Slowly your view of a situation will begin to change, giving place to a new perspective, a changed outlook. You may begin to realize that certain things that seemed crucial are not as important as you thought, whereas others that you had not even considered now seem to be vital."33

Phillip Keller warns, "It takes time, a lot of time, precious time, to listen, to hear, to understand, 'to see' what He is saying. Most of us are slow of spirit, preoccupied with our petty pursuits and petty pride. We are not sensitive to His Spirit speaking to us in His Word. Too often we are preoccupied with the workaday world and whirl of pleasure around us."34

Friends, there seems to be no way around it: no shortcut. If we want to know God's will and His guidance for our lives, we are going to have to take time to still our hearts and minds in quietness before Him and listen. But then, time is His greatest gift to us. What better way could there be to use it than this. Let's spend time with God and receive His direction for what is ahead – one hour, one day at a time. We won't be disappointed.

A Call, a Heifer and the Soo

What could a young cow possibly have to do with a life of ministry? A lot! While a very young teen I received a clear call of God to invest my life in full-time ministry. That was the vision. The rest was a matter of working out the details. An unknown author penned the words, "The will of God will not lead you where the grace of God cannot keep you." In the midst of the risky unknowingness of that call there was an underlying confidence that God would provide all my needs. When my high school years ended, the test came.

The first step was a decision to leave my family home, move 350 miles away to Sault Ste. Marie, Ontario (affectionately known as "The Soo") to attend a technical college for one year before then moving on to Bible college. God had guided me to study geology that year in order to provide skills for further work that would fund my ministerial training. The direction was clear. How to make it happen was the risky part.

I grew up on a 100-acre mixed farm where extra money was scarce or non-existent. However, in his efforts to teach his three sons some entrepreneurial and business skills, my Dad had given each of us a calf to raise and eventually sell. This was our project. We had to do all the work of caring for it. When the time arrived for me to leave for college, my calf had grown into a young heifer. Selling this animal was the only resource I had to provide my college tuition. I knew the exact amount needed. With fear and trembling I hired our neighbor to truck my heifer to the weekly auction sale. The trucking cost was now added to the tuition amount.

If you have ever participated in an auction you know how nerve-wracking it can be. Will the bids reach the level you need? You can only watch and hang on. Finally, my animal was brought into the ring and the bidding started. The bids rose, then slowed. I knew the needed amount: $175. It was at the upper end of my animal's worth. Bidding, however, stalled around the $160 mark.

One trick I had heard of (I was extremely nervous and brand new at this) was to bid on my own animal in an effort to raise the purchase price. I did this once, and then twice, when to my dismay the other bidder stopped. I had bought my animal back!! Now what? I made nothing and on top of that now had to pay the auction fees and trucking fees with money I did not have. I was deflated.

My neighbor-trucker was a wise and experienced man. He leaned over and had a brief conversation with the farmer who had been bidding on my heifer. I never knew exactly what was said. But my friend turned back to me and informed me that the other farmer had agreed to buy my heifer at my bidding price. Whew! What relief! I was redeemed. God had supplied. I was able to pay the extra fees. I had exactly enough left to cover my tuition. With that provision, I left for the Soo and launched out on the journey that would eventually include eleven years of post-secondary and graduate studies and 38 years of pastoral and para-church ministry. God is good.

Are you trembling at the risk of following the will of God in your life? Take courage. Step out in faith. He will provide for you. I know.

God's Timing

"I want it now – better yet, yesterday!" Is this not the spirit of our age? We want instant gratification; not waiting for anything. Spoiled or what? Yet, even a moment's reflection reminds us that this is not the way life works. There is a lot of waiting. This reality is biblically true. In the biblical book of Ecclesiastes, we read: *"There is a time for everything, and a season for every activity under heaven"* and, *"He has made everything beautiful in its time"* (vs. 1, 11). God works with a long perspective, accomplishing His ultimate purposes in His perfect time. Let me illustrate that with two instances from my own life.

As a 12-year old child I had a profound sense of God calling me to give my life in service to Him. The first whisper to my inner consciousness was the question, "Ross, will you be a missionary for me?" My immediate response was, "Yes Lord." The direction of my life was set. As time progressed, I felt added to that call the impressions, "Will you be a missionary to India?" and later, "will you be a missionary pilot to India?" There were influences working on my life; a godly pastor who had been a Salvation Army missionary to India and the book, *Jungle Pilot*, which recounted the lives of five young missionaries, one a pilot, killed by the Auca Indians in Ecuador. These were formative in sorting out the mystery of God's call on my life. In time, my attempts at fulfilling the pilot part of the calling terminated with a specialist's diagnosis of nerve deafness in one ear that ended my nine-hour flying career. During my Bible college years God clearly steered me into a lifetime of pastoring. But what of the "missionary to India" part of that call? Here's where we come to God's timing.

In 2013 I flew to Bangalore, India to be the guest (missionary) speaker at an Indian Bible College's Missions Conference, Graduation Ceremony and other events. It took almost fifty years to get there, but God's timing is perfect ... and, beautiful! As I prepared for that trip, I reflected on the great influence a number of East Indian people and missionaries to India had on my life. I've was reminded of how God works faithfully to accomplish His purposes in His time. John Wesley in his *Explanatory Notes* on those Ecclesiastes verses wrote: "Purpose – Not only natural, but even the voluntary actions of men, are ordered and disposed by God."

My second instance goes back to 1983. My wife Bev and I had been married twelve years. Infertility had prevented us from bearing our own children and a long adoption process finally ended. In February of that year a beautiful 12-day-old baby girl was placed in our arms and our lives were forever changed. The night before the call came we had attended a Valentine's banquet. The guest musician sang the song, "In His time, In His time, He makes all things beautiful in His time!" We have now celebrated Heidi's 34th birthday and rejoice in the three precious granddaughters she and her husband Ryan have given us. God also enabled us to adopt two toddlers from Romania in 1990 who are also now grown adults. Ecclesiastes 3:1 and 11 are true. Are you struggling with God's timing in your life? Be patient. He is at work! He knows what He is doing for you so you can fulfill His mission for your life.

Fair Havens

"Three times I was shipwrecked. Once I spent a whole night and a day adrift at sea" (2 Corinthians11:25). Here's a guy who probably shouldn't go on a cruise! Right Paul?! Paul's last shipwreck on the Isle of Malta may be one of the most famous of all time. Having appealed to Caesar for the right to defend himself against his Jewish accusers, Paul was being taken to Rome to face trial. It was a long and arduous journey. With winter setting in, the Roman troop caught a ship hoping to make it to a safe harbour. It was not to be. The ship did make it safely to Fair Havens but just a little further on was the larger, safer port of Phoenix. An argument arose over whether to stay or go. Maybe the sailors were thinking there would be more to do in the larger port, better protection, better entertainment and better beer to drink for a whole winter. Who knows? So, against Paul's better advice, they set out and lost everything except their lives on that reef strewn coast.

Steven P. Wickstrom observed that: "The parallel in our own lives is staggering. Sometimes (quite often, actually) God says NO to us. It is not always because what we ask for, or what we want to do is unreasonable or bad for us. It may be because the journey to get there is too hazardous. God often tells us to wait because the weather outside is not right for the journey. I don't think that there was a bubble of fair weather sitting on top of Fair Havens. The crew of the ship knew what the weather was like, yet they decided to sail anyway. We have a tendency to be the same way, we hear God's voice warning us to wait, and decide that we know better. We set our sails and steer straight into the storms of life. Have you ever done that? Have you ever gone against the will of God and wondered why life suddenly got so rough? I know I have. Sometimes I wonder if I'll ever learn to truly trust God. Maybe you have the same problem. Sometimes we go through in life what Paul's shipmates are about to go through in the storm."[35]

Are you needing to make a decision about something right now? To go or to stay? What do you sense God is saying to you?

What is your heart wanting to do? What about your desires and emotions? Are the two directions in line or do you find an inner battle going on as you resist God's guidance? How often have you been there?! Take a break. Take time to relax, refresh, make new friends and admire God's beautiful creation all around. Perhaps it might also be a time to seriously pray through with God the direction you are wrestling with, or even more, to approach God about why this heart of yours is so rebellious towards doing his will. May he lead you into a place of Fair Havens as you do so.

Seasons in Time

November 22, 1963 most of the world came to a stop as news flashed across the airwaves of the assassination of U.S. President John F. Kennedy in Dallas, Texas. Not long ago we commemorated the 50th anniversary of that event which marked the generation of which I am a part. My parents' generation was branded in a similar way by the Japanese bombing of Pearl Harbor in Hawaii on December 7, 1941, an event that propelled the USA into World War II. A younger generation was similarly impacted by the bombing of the World Trade Center in New York City on September 11, 2001 – now known for all time as 9/11. Pervasive conditions in a society can also mark a culture. The Israelites in the time of the Judges were marked by the general attitude recorded in Judges 17:6: *In those days there was no king in Israel; everyone did what was right in his own eyes.* Single events in time and all-pervasive attitudes can make an imprint on a society that characterizes it for all time.

There is another reference to time that carries a similar import that touches us even today. It is found in Galatians 4:4: *"But when the fullness of the time came, God sent forth his Son …"*

It's the Christmas story. 'In the fullness of time' – when everything was exactly right – when all the conditions were perfect – in that moment in time God sent His one and only Son into the world to accomplish the Father's plan to redeem lost mankind and bring us back into relationship with Him. The circumstances making this 'the fullness of time' are fascinating: the pervasion of Greek culture throughout the Roman Empire that brought together three continents under the *Pax Romana* – the Roman rule of peace; one common trade language spoken throughout the empire – the *koine* Greek; the amazing Roman-built road system that connected the furthest reaches of the empire; the readiness of the Jewish people for the arrival of their Messiah; all of these and many more made the time for His coming perfect and enabled the rapid spread of the Gospel's good news throughout the world.

73

One-time historical events can impact a generation broadly. Universal conditions throughout a culture can change a generation markedly. Are we aware of them, ready to respond to them and eager to make the most of every opportunity, redeeming "the time" that is upon us (Ephesians 5:15-16)? In a similar way, arriving in our lives at the season known as the senior years or the second half of life is a significant time that marks us and carries great opportunity. As hard as it may be to admit it, we are no longer young. We are no longer even middle-aged. We are now mature elders, the seniors in the land. For each of us this is a time of great import. Now the question remains: what are we going to do (for God and others) in this season of life? We each bring a unique host of memories, skills, experiences, strengths and abilities to this life stage. Let's dedicate them to God and make the most of this opportune "time" to bless our world where God has placed us to reflect His glory.

Rhythms of Life

The Apostle Paul knew what it was to be exhausted. *"I have labored and toiled and have often gone without sleep,"* he reported (2 Corinthians 11:27). He went on to recount all he had endured and suffered in his efforts to serve his Lord in sharing the good news of Christ's salvation (vs. 23-33). It would be easy to let guilt drive us to a non-stop lifestyle of ministry if we read only this passage and tried to copy Paul. I must do more – better, faster! But this is only one-half the story. It must be balanced by God's command in Psalm 46:10, *"Be still, and know that I am God,"* and the example of Jesus Himself when he told His disciples, *"Come with me by yourselves to a quiet place and get some rest."*

Do you ever struggle with a need for balance in your life? Do you feel guilty if you stop, take a "time out" and do nothing except 'veg' or rest? Don't! (Unless, of course, you do that *all* of the time)! The truth is, there must be rhythms to our lives. There are seasons when we do go all out in work and service. Yes. However, these must be balanced by periods of rest, renewal and re-creating. Every moment we are reminded of this necessary balance. We breathe in. Then, we must breathe out. We cannot do only one. Every breath in must be matched with a breath out. That is the reality of life. We violate those rhythms at our own peril.

My wife Bev and I frequently go through seasons when life is full. Intense service, interspersed with weekly assignments, visits from our precious children and granddaughters, and many social events, followed by looming deadlines. One can become addicted to the adrenaline rush of all this. We certainly come to the point of the exhaustion of St. Paul. However, no one can maintain this pace 24/7, 365 days of the year. No one! Not indefinitely. To attempt to do so is simply to schedule a pending health failure, nervous collapse, or a fall into depression. It's not a matter of 'if,' but 'when.' The antidote is the regular observance of a Sabbath day's rest, periodic times where productivity is put on hold, and an occasional 'veg' or rest day indulgence with no guilt allowed! Just do it! And while you do, open yourself to breathe in the Lord's presence. Invite Him to renew your soul. By the way, 'veg' is short for vegetate. Even when plants seem to be doing nothing – vegging – they are actually growing, taking in, giving out and preparing to bear fruit. As will you.

Often in spring my wife and I schedule ourselves to take a ferry to an island retreat center just off our British Columbia coast, to spend three days with other ministry leaders. We enjoy the ambiance of beautifully-decorated rooms, delicious meals, spectacular scenery and a few encouraging input sessions from great ministry leaders. We have time to rest, be with each other and renew. We know we need it and so we schedule it. Each year we can hardly wait. How about you? Do you dare to make time to renew? Don't fight it. Get in touch with the rhythms of life.

Take a Vacation. Yes, You!

Ahh, vacation. Extended time off from your primary vocation, job or full routine of servanthood commitments in the retirement years. You don't have to deserve it; you simply need it. Yes, you. Every single one of us (without exceptions) needs time away to renew and re-create!

As I wrote this we were staying in a hotel in Kenora, Ontario. We had already enjoyed a week of camping by a lake near Vernon, BC, accompanied for five of those days by our precious then 2- and 4-year-old granddaughters and Makita, our grand dog. After that we journeyed to Calgary, Regina and then, Kenora, motelling and camping along the way. Eventually we arrived at our destination of Thunder Bay where we spent over a week camping and visiting with my wife's mother and siblings and their families. Oh yes, I did work a little when I officiated at our niece's wedding. But for the most part, this was summer "holidays" (the term we use in Canada for vacation). I was fully committed to unwinding and enjoying this time with a completely free conscience, knowing we needed this break.

Yet I know some reading this, struggle with the whole idea of down time: days off, time off, vacations. They feel they must always be "on duty", always working, always being productive and striving to prove their worth and earn time away. There is a "classic Greek term" for this attitude (or was it Hebrew?). It is, "hogwash!!"

You don't believe me? Well argue with this fact. Jesus' entire public ministry lasted only three years before his crucifixion. So how important was it to him to work constantly, 24-7, to accomplish everything he had to in such a short time? After an incredibly intense time of ministry by him and his disciples, *"He said unto them, Come ye yourselves apart into a desert place, and rest a while: for there were many coming and going, and they had no leisure so much as to eat"* (Mark 6:31, KJV). Jesus knew the importance of rest and commanded it. Someone has rightly said: "Come ye apart ... or you will come apart!"

Anytime I think of this topic I remember words of Oswald Sanders that I read over 25 years ago. "It is possible to throw our lives away foolishly by burning the candle at both ends. When Robert Murray McCheyne, only thirty years old, lay dying, he said to a friend at his bedside, 'God gave me a message to deliver and a horse to ride. Alas, I killed the horse, and now I cannot deliver the message.' The horse was, of course, his body. Christian workers should accept it that their service will be costly if it is to be effective, but they should be careful not to kill the horse."[36] I am also reminded of a book written by Christian counselor, Wayne Oates, entitled: *Workaholics, Make Laziness Work for You*. Isn't that a great title?! He advocates finding ways to rest, renew and re-create even in the midst of very full ministry and work lives. I hope I've convinced you that it's okay to take time off. Just do it.

φ

Chapter 7

FAITH, TRUST AND SURRENDER

Practical Atheists!

"Lord, I believe. Help my unbelief" (Mark 9:24). Aren't those sentiments familiar? Expressed by the father of a dumb, demonized son brought to Jesus for healing and deliverance, they came in response to Christ's declaration that *"everything is possible for one who believes"* (Mark 9:23). "I believe, I think, but do I really? Does my life demonstrate that I do?" I empathize with that hopeful-doubting father.

Years ago, while preparing a sermon, I came across a commentator who used the phrase "practical atheist."[37] I was intrigued by his concept. He was referring to people who called themselves Christians and yet who worried, fretted, feared and acted as if there were no such reality as a God who knew them, cared for them and was able to do exceedingly abundantly beyond all they ask or even imagine (Eph. 3:20). They failed to pray and trust and lived their "Christian lives" as if there were no powerful God at work in them and for them. Wow! I've never been able to get away from that convicting image. I wonder am I the only one who slides into such a trap?

Recently I came across the term *apatheist* which describes a similar reality. Vernon Grounds defines this as "the multitude who are theists but are indifferent to God in daily living. ... *apatheists.* That word is built on the noun *apathy,* which means 'indifference,' a sort of sluggish unconcern. And sadly, whatever belief an individual professes, he may be living as an apatheist. His faith may make only a minimal difference in his behavior."[38] Have we fallen into that ditch?

God has a remedy. It's called *trust* and *thankfulness*! Every day God calls us to go to the deepest center of our being where He resides, and act in trust and thankfulness. Trust keeps us from worry and obsessing; thankfulness keeps us from the sister sins of criticizing and complaining! "It is a free choice that you must make thousands of times daily. The more you choose to trust Me, the easier it becomes. Thought patterns of trust become etched into your brain" says the Lord to us.[39]

In choosing "trust" I choose against "worry" which, for the true believer, is both *irrelevant* and *irreverent*![40] Irrelevant because worry alters nothing! Have you ever once been able to worry yourself out of one single problem you faced?! Never. I've fretted myself into a stew but never out of one! Irreverent because it declares we do not trust God and His promises to us (therefore, declaring ourselves to be practical atheists!). So, I'm left with one positive act: choose to believe in who God says He is and what He says he can do and to trust Him with thanksgiving. Won't you join me?! I sure don't want us to be known as practical atheists based on how we live.

Balanced Faith

A church I was once part of engaged in a corporate study of "Daring Faith: The Key to Miracles."[41] For forty days we examined many aspects of a daily faith in God that goes beyond the norm, stretching our trust and obedience. It was stimulating! We considered expressions of a faith on one hand, which is no faith at all; commitments in familiar, well-tested environments with no reach required. That was in contrast to extreme acts which are presumptive and ill thought out, demanding God do something beyond common sense and the orderly way in which His universe operates. Somewhere in the middle range of these two extremes is where true faith can be put to the test in daring ways.

I thought back to a time in my life where I had been daring. As a first-year college student studying to be a geology technician I sent out over seventy resumes in my search for summer work in this field. That was in the pre-email days of typewriters, copiers and snail mail. I succeeded in landing a role in uranium exploration working in the northern Ontario wilderness. Employed by a small subsidiary of a major corporation, I made my way to North Bay to begin my new job. From there we drove for two days to Red Lake, Ontario, our jumping off point for the summer. As a lad of 19 I met my summer work partner, a seasoned old claim-staker, George, who was probably in his fifties – though I remember him as seeming to be much more ancient than that. From the float plane base in Red Lake we were flown over 100 miles north and dropped off to do magnetometer ground readings of aerial-surveyed radioactive hot spots. George's job was to get us where we needed to go, keep us alive and prevent us from getting lost. Mine was to measure and record the instrument readings over the ground we covered.

I look back now and see the venture as totally daring. Bush flying, camping in bear and wild animal country and travelling on foot or by canoe, we were totally out of contact between the pre-arranged pick-up and re-location dates. Talk about daily faith! I remember having a near-heart attack one day when a towering moose suddenly broke cover from the deadfall where it had been standing motionless and undetected as I approached. Fortunately, it ran away and did not charge towards me. Be still my beating heart! Then there were the bears. But those are stories for another time.

Our transportation between search locations was accomplished in single-engine bush planes. Consider the faith of those pilots who daily flew over vast uncharted wilderness with no navigational aids in those days other than what they spotted on the ground as they compared the maps held on their laps. True, in event of an engine failure they could land on water with their pontoon equipped craft. But if they went down no one would be coming soon to their aid. I remember one young recently trained pilot in his early twenties who mixed his new faith-filled career of bush flying with substantial amounts of caution and common sense. From one narrow, rather short lake, he opted to fly my partner and I out one at a time with half of our gear on each flight. I was left behind as he flew George, our canoe and some of our belongings to the next lake we would be working from. Fortunately, he did return for me an hour later and we had a safe transition. His was a daring faith, mixed with an appropriate understanding of safe parameters. What was my faith takeaway from this experience? Yes, we are to risk and overcome fear as we step out in faith. However, we are to do so within the understanding of the character and workings of God and not be foolish and presumptive. May our faith be stretched in such ways.

No Fear!

We live in an era when it is easy to be intimidated by fear! Our daily news is filled with events that inspire fear. It comes from many quarters. Another suicide bombing is reported in the Middle East, claiming even more lives. Reports of a tragic mass shooting somewhere in North America fill our TV screens. Political races with candidates continually talking about the threat of terrorism or nuclear warfare and if elected, what they will do to stop it, bombard our ears. The news of another friend or family member diagnosed with cancer or a fatal illness shakes us to the core. The breakup of another marriage and disruption of a family, friends of ours, leave us wondering about the security of our own relationships. A mugging, or abduction, or shooting in our neighbourhoods make us fearful to go out. Need I go on? The threats shake us every day.

What is fear? There is a continuum of fear that runs from doubt or uncertainty through a nameless sense of anxiety to an extreme emotion of sheer terror and panic. Oxford defines the noun fear variously as, an unpleasant emotion caused by the threat of danger, pain or harm, to a feeling of anxiety concerning the outcome of something or safety of someone, to the likelihood of something unwelcome happening. The archaic meaning was a mixed feeling of dread and reverence, as in, "to fear God." The verb fear implies being afraid of someone or something as likely to be dangerous, painful or harmful and therefore to feel anxiety on behalf of someone or something. I almost hesitate to bring this subject up and describe it for I may be creating a sense of fear in you just by writing about it!

How in the world do we live with this prevalent fear and not go crazy! Good question! Let's begin by stating an obvious truth. Fear is not new or unique to our twenty-first century. I know we are often told it is, but, it is not! The reasons for fear may have multiplied but there have always been life-threatening, world-shattering events that have provoked mankind to fear. Our loving God knows this and has given us good counsel so we'll know how to live in the midst of it. His words for us work, yes, even in the extremes of our day. Here I speak especially to those who know Jesus Christ as their Savior and live in a saving relationship with Him each day.

Christians in biblical times faced world threats, war, health issues, bondage, oppression, death, and above all that, persecution because they believed in and obeyed God. Warren Wiersbe reminds us that "Christ is praying for us and will soon come to take us home. The secret is faith. Doubt and fear always go together, and **faith and peace always go together**. May we not be 'little-faith' Christians!"[42] Jesus spoke words to his disciples that are for believers of every age. We should not be frightened by national, international, and natural calamities, or give up when persecution becomes intense. Times of tribulation can be times of testimony, and the Spirit will give us the wisdom and words that we need. Because we know what will happen, we can be ready to meet it. On several crisis occasions, the Lord appeared to Paul to sustain him and to assure him that He was with him and would give him many converts. In the storm, Christ assured Paul that He would not forsake him. We wonder if Paul leaned heavily on Psalm 23:4, *"Yea, though I walk through the valley of the shadow of death, I will fear no evil; for Thou art with me (KJV)."* Whether or not Paul did, we can – and must! Fear not friends! Christ is in us and will be with us, always, no matter what!

"Unbroken"

He was born 17 days after my father and only 290 miles away. Name: Louis Silvie Zamperini. I first heard about him from our California cousins one spring after he had shared his testimony at their church. Then he was ninety-four and still going strong. That should not be surprising. But for the advent of World War II he was headed to be the first man to break the four-minute mile. As a winning Olympian, he shook the hand of Hitler at the Olympic Games in Berlin in 1936. His future was filled with promise of untold athletic achievements to come.

World War II changed all that. Enrolled in the air force and trained as a bombardier, his B-24 was shot down in May, 1943. Only three men survived the crash into the Pacific Ocean. For the next forty-seven days Louis floated aimlessly, fending off sharks, suffered strafing by a Japanese Zero pilot who put 48 bullet holes in their life raft, blazing sun, chilling nights, and lack of food and water. One of the men died at sea. At one point Louis called out to God for rain, promising to give his life to Him if He answered – and God did! Yet for many years Louis' promise lay forgotten.

Finally, they reached land – only to be captured by Japanese soldiers. The next months in internment camps could only be described as "hell on earth" for Louis. Yet throughout, he remained *Unbroken*, the title given to the story on his life written by Laura Hillenbrand, author also of *Seabiscuit*.[43] Liberation came in August, 1944. However, Louis would not be back home until October.

The torture took a severe toll. Memories of his inhumane slavery and torture, especially by one particularly vicious prison camp commander, brought on flashbacks, nightmares and terror that led to alcoholism, the near-break-up of his marriage and suicidal depression. A life once so promising looked like it would end in abysmal failure.

But God! Fall, 1949 Billy Graham extended his Los Angeles crusade a few extra weeks. Near the end of this time Louis Zamperini was pressured by his wife to attend two times. He determined that at the altar call on the second night, he would get up and leave, never to return. Instead, the life-transforming power of God's Holy Spirit broke through and he was literally, born-again! Peace flooded his being. The flashbacks never returned! This "walking dead man" found new purpose in caring for his family and a host of lost youth over the ensuing decades. He was still going strong for God for years after, fulfilling the promise made on a life raft in the Pacific Ocean years before.

Has your life been tough? Any promises you made to God remaining unfulfilled? Do you have some good reasons (excuses?) as to why you can't honor those God-surrenders or God-commitments you made in the past? If so, how do they stack up alongside what Louis Zamperini endured? Maybe you don't have as much reason to not follow God as you thought, eh? Why not get back on track with Christ? It's not too late and God can and will use you too, well into older age. Make a fresh start today.

Φ

Chapter 8

SERVING, PRAYING

Volunteer, or Servant?

In 1979, famous musician Bob Dylan sang the words, "You're gonna have to serve somebody, yes indeed, You're gonna have to serve somebody, Well, it may be the devil or it may be the Lord, But you're gonna have to serve somebody." Yes indeed! Or, maybe not? Maybe not if instead of "serving," you "volunteer!"

In our culture, we tend to volunteer but think of it as serving. But are they the same thing? A gal named Jamie Arpin-Ricci ran a used bookstore in Winnipeg as an outreach ministry of Youth With A Mission. It was a warm place that attracted a lot of youth to special activities during lunch hours and after school. The kids really connected with the volunteers who hung out with them. But then, the partnering organization pulled out, taking their volunteers with them. The kids couldn't figure out why their "friends" had left them. One little girl said to them: "This is the third kids program where people just left us. They were Christians too."

Volunteers can do that. Volunteering is usually done for a season while it works for one's schedule. It usually has good motivations behind it – one wants to do something good for people, a group or an organization. But volunteerism is not the same as servanthood. Servants of Jesus Christ are disciples who hear the call to take up their cross daily and follow Him. This is a calling – a fulfillment of our destiny. It is on a higher plane. In servanthood, there are no high or low tasks. All are equal before God. In the words of English poet, Robert Browning: "All service ranks the same with God: With God, whose puppets, best and worst, Are we, there is no last nor first."

Have you stopped to review what you do in your church or community? In your "spare" time? In serving or volunteering? Which category would it fall into? How are you investing your life? There is a sense to volunteering in which we choose to remain "in control." I determine when, how much, and when I'll quit. A lot of it is about "me." In servanthood, it is all about serving Christ in His kingdom and for His glory.

However, there is a great benefit to this. It was described by one of my dear Seminary professors, Dr. Ralph Earle, who himself modeled a lifestyle of servanthood that often moved me. He wrote: "... Herein lies a paradox: The more we serve others, the more free we find we actually are. For in loving service to others we are freed from the self-centeredness that is actually the worst slavery."[44] I don't know if we realize this, but in deciding to serve we set ourselves free from becoming a self-centered, self-focused individual. And in the process, we make ourselves beloved to all we serve.

There is one additional benefit. It's in the way Jesus now sees us: *"I no longer call you servants, because a servant does not know his master's business. Instead, I have called you friends, for everything that I learned from my Father I have made known to you"* (John 15:15). Hey, I want to be more than just a volunteer. I want to be a friend of Jesus. Don't you? Let's serve.

Prompted to Pray

A great privilege believers in Jesus Christ enjoy is having other Christians praying for them. In ways we may not fully see or understand, this makes incredible differences for the better in us. We are blessed. But, for those who serve in full-time vocational Christian ministry, this is not simply a blessing they enjoy. This is indispensable for their very survival. They have an enemy who relentlessly works to take them out. He knows that if a leader falls, the resulting kingdom devastation will be exponential in its impact. They absolutely must have God's people praying for them if they are to last in the work to which God calls them. Sometimes we are not fully aware of how crucial is such a prayer cover.

An incredible blessing in ministry is to have prayer warriors who commit to praying for you every day. I can hardly believe anyone would do that. And yet, I have had such people in my life: seven to be exact (that I know of). I really have no idea, and will not until eternity, of what disasters their prayers have saved me from across the years. How many times were the enemy's strategies and schemes to kill, steal and destroy, defeated by the prayers of these saints? I do not know. But, I'm aware they were. I am grateful. However, I am also concerned. Four of my daily prayer warriors have gone home to heaven. My dear "father figure" from college days died in 2010. My mother went home in 2012. My prayer cover is lessening. The dear lady who came to the Lord in my first pastorate assures me every time I talk to her that she still prays for me daily 36 years later! Recently I met a dear saint in her 90's from a pastorate of over a dozen years ago. She informed me that she still prays for me every day! Unbelievable! I am humbled by the commitment of these remaining three saints. But I know I need others. I may have them, though I don't know about them. I pray this to be so. I pray it is true for you as well.

Some seniors enter into a phase wherein they struggle to find meaningful purpose for their lives. "All I can do now is pray," they may sigh in resignation. I want to elevate that ministry to a new level. This is not an "all I can do now" thing. This is an incredible calling that may mean the difference between survival or falling for pastors, missionaries, evangelists or other Christian workers. A daily practice of prayer, covering a worker, may turn out to be one of the highest rewarded callings in the Kingdom to come! Intercession is far from easy. It will stretch you! Yet what a difference you could make even if wheelchair-bound or bed-ridden. Your prayers are powerful. Are you prompted to take up the challenge of covering your pastor, your missionary, or your family members in prayer? Oh, please act on this prompting! Make the commitment and engage in daily, systematic intercessory prayer for those God places on your heart. This may become the most significant investment you will have made in your entire life. Your children, grandchildren, pastors and friends need you!

Alfred, Lord Tennyson wrote these powerful words:

> *"Pray for my soul. More things are wrought by prayer*
> *Than this world dreams of.*
> *Wherefore, let thy voice Rise like a fountain*
> *for me night and day. ..."*[45]

Christian Education

We live in a culture which has long placed a high value on education. Education can provide a lift to elevate a person from a dead-end future to a hopeful one. Bishop Nelson Mandela is quoted as saying, "Education is the most powerful weapon which you can use to change the world." Education has always been important in Christianity. That explains why many of the greatest universities of our society were in fact founded as centers for the training of ministers to preach the gospel and serve mankind. Harvard, Princeton, McGill – name the school, go back to its roots and this is most likely what you will find. Sadly, over time secular humanism co-opted these schools and took them over. At the same time, it appears to me, there has been a growing trend within the church to downplay and even ignore the vital importance of Christian education for believers. This is to abandon our roots.

The Old Testament's clearest teaching, known as the *Shema* (Deuteronomy 6:4-9), gave specific guidelines for instructing children in the faith. In the New Testament Jesus included this mandate in the Great Commission – *"teaching them to obey everything I have commanded you"* (Matthew 28:16-20). The apostle Paul, himself trained by the greatest teachers of his day, urged Timothy and other leaders to carefully instruct believers in the most holy faith. The Bereans were held up as an example because they did not accept anything Paul taught until they first carefully compared it to the Scriptures to ensure that it rang true (Acts 17:11).

The need for thorough Christian education, now frequently called discipleship or spiritual formation, has not passed. Yet why is there so little of it? It is not that it has been tried and found wanting. Rather, it is because it has been tried and found hard and was therefore ignored!

William Barclay wrote, "It's possible to be a follower of Jesus without being a disciple; to be a camp-follower without being a soldier of the king; to be a hanger-on in some great work without pulling one's weight. Once someone was talking to a great scholar about a younger man. He said, 'So and so tells me that he was one of your students.' The teacher answered devastatingly, 'He may have attended my lectures, but he was not one of my students.' There is a world of difference between attending lectures and being a student. It is one of the supreme handicaps of the Church that in the Church there are so many distant followers of Jesus and so few real disciples"[46]

As a student of the Word who completed a Masters degree in Christian Education, I long for a return to making this a priority for every believer in the church. Oh, that every follower of Christ would commit to diligently study and be led in laying personal foundations of faith understanding so that they would "correctly handle the word of truth" (2 Timothy 2:15). Join me in this. Perhaps together we can start a revolution of Christian education in today's Church and thereby improve the level of serving!

φ

Chapter 9

GOD'S GRACE AND LOVE

Oceans of Grace

Alaska. What an amazing place – at least the small portion the senior's Alaska cruise group that I led, saw of it one month. Of course, to my mind, the Alaskan Panhandle should really be a part of the province of British Columbia, Canada since it borders BC all the way north! I even learned that Whitehorse N.W.T. (Northwest Territories) is approximately the same latitude as Anchorage. And did you know that Juneau, the capital of Alaska has absolutely NO roads leading in or out of it and that one-half of the 27,000 or so residents are all employed by various government agencies?! The only way to get there is by water or air!

Our group of 26 people shared many wonderful times getting to know each other better, strengthening relationships amongst the group's members and a few new friends who joined us. When one calculates the value of accommodations, exquisite daily meals, varied entertainment and tourism opportunities, enjoyment of our own meeting room and refreshments each day, etc. it was quite an inexpensive way to spend seven days together. I think that most all who went can hardly wait for another travel experience like that one!

One of the main highlights for all was the daily ministry. Many shared their faith in Jesus Christ with crew members and fellow passengers. Each day we were challenged to leave the sweet fragrance of Jesus Christ with everyone we met. A wonderful couple from Australia heard about our daily chapels before we even boarded the ship and joined our group every day, adding a whole new dimension to our lives. The daily testimonies in our chapel time ranged from the account of a missionary couple who lost their 15-year-old son to a crocodile in Africa, to an account of a dramatic healing from cancer, to musical ministry with a harmonica. These encouraged everyone to grow closer to the Lord.

The theme, *"Oceans of God's Grace,"* each day provided a vehicle for reflecting on the awesome aspects of the oceans that cover the major portion of our earth's surface and how they illustrate the character of God and His wonderful work in our lives. Lessons from Philip Keller's *Sea Edge* opened new windows of light into God's Word. The unstoppable, continual action of the tides, of the breakers scouring the shorelines, and of the healing and cleansing of the salty sea, revealed to us the inexorable work of God in the hearts and lives of those who trust in Him. However, we learned that we can also build breakwaters around our lives to keep God under control in us. When we do this, we shut the wild, uncontrollable God out of our lives and turn our hearts into stagnant cesspools that may look placid on the surface but underneath are contaminated by selfishness and legalistic bondage. We were dared to trust God fully and to let this mighty God have full sway in every dimension of our lives. Like the breathtaking oceans which are more majestic than we can begin to comprehend, is our astounding God who can do more in us and for us than we can dare dream. What a privilege it was to grow together! This growth is for each of us every day. Let God loose in your life!

Chesed Love

Diane Cameron observed, "February is to winter what Wednesday is to the work week." It's that bleak mid-winter month with no long weekend holiday in sight. However, February does have one redeeming quality (besides Ground Hog Day!): Valentine's. Ah, the month for love. Love can transform the bleakest human situation.

His name was Alvin Lawhead. A pastor turned Bible college professor. Later he became "Dr." Lawhead and went on to teach at the seminary. As a single man in his early forties he came to our Bible College to teach Old Testament for a brief tenure. Loving and caring, he evidenced a pastor's heart toward students. What has stuck with me most through all these years was his instruction on God's *chesed* (pronounced 'hesed') love. A Hebrew word used multiple times, it is hard to fully translate. Usually it comes across in English as "steadfast" or "long-suffering." Also, as "mercy" and "loving-kindness." Yet it is even more than all those words convey. Dr. Lawhead's entire countenance would warm to the task of trying to explain this love. He must have gone back to it frequently for in my mind, memory of him equates with *chesed* love. What is this love God has for us?

This *chesed* love or mercy brings relief to at least five different *miseries* common to life. When we are treated unfairly by life or people and are tempted to resentment, God's mercy will relieve us from the misery of *bitterness*. As we grieve the heart-rending loss of a dearly loved person from our life through death, God's mercy will relieve us from the misery of *anger* which may come in reaction to the loss. If we find ourselves living with the limitations of a handicap it will be God's *chesed* mercy that relieves us from the misery of *self-pity*. What about pain? When we are hurting physically and face the misery of *hopelessness* it will only be God's mercy that keeps us from being overwhelmed by affliction. Finally, there is sin: personal sin which is our common lot in life and which can be overwhelmingly debilitating. It is God's steadfast, unconditional love that relieves the misery of *guilt*. What's more, His mercies come new every morning! In Chuck Swindoll's words, "No unfair consequence is too extreme for mercy. No grief too deep. No handicap too debilitating. No pain too excruciating. No sin too shameful." Wow!

Many years have passed since my exposure to Dr. Lawhead's *chesed* love of Old Testament vintage. I have needed that long-suffering, steadfast, loving-kindness mercy in my life time and time again. God has not failed. He has loved me in this way in every season of my need.

Does God truly love you in this way? Let Max Lucado answer that. "Picture a dump truck full of love. There you are behind it. God lifts the bed until the love starts to slide. Slowly at first, then down, down, down until you are hidden, buried, covered in this love." This month open your life to be buried in God's *chesed* love.

"No Longer A Prisoner: Forgiveness"

Refusal to forgive makes a prisoner ... of you! This is counterintuitive, yet true. My refusal to forgive a person who deeply hurt or offended me may be my way to tie them up so their lives suffer some hurt for what they did to me. Or, so I think. The reality is completely different. The offender may be totally oblivious to my ill will and unforgiveness. However, I will become a prisoner of my own bitterness. I may not even realize it has happened. I only know my life is becoming harder, darker and more constricted as each day passes. Something is terribly off and I'm not even sure what it is. Do you find yourself there today? Be honest? Are you a prisoner of your own making?

Walden said "unforgiveness is like a scratch on an old record [for those of you who remember those!]. The song never goes on to the end, it keeps the beautiful music yet to be released, unheard and all that resounds is the same old three or four chords again and again and again." How dare they did that to me. How dare they did that to me. How dare they ...

My late shepherd friend, Philip Keller observed: "our human inability fully to forgive others who have wronged us leads to most of the trouble and trauma of our brief sojourn on earth. We will not freely forgive those who trespass on our rights or trample on our personal pride. We hold men and women to ransom. We demand our pound of flesh as proper recompense."[47] What we do not realize is that in refusing to forgive we imprison ourselves by our very unforgiveness.

But, forgiveness is so beautiful. Two of my favourite words in Scripture are "... and Peter." What, you say?! Yes. In Mark 16:7 after he rose from the dead and appeared to the women in the garden Jesus instructed them, *"But go, tell his disciples and Peter. ..."* Why did he add those two extra words? Was Peter not a disciple? He was. Yet Jesus knew the deep shame Peter would be feeling for having denied His Lord three times. He wanted Peter to know he forgave him. This special direction would communicate to Peter that he held nothing against him. He was fully forgiven. As a result, Peter was transformed.

Forgiveness does not mean forgetting what has been done and allowing the offender to hurt you again. When trust has been broken, it will need to be rebuilt. That is not automatic. But forgiveness allows the sting of the wrong to be removed. The costly shedding of Christ's blood for all sin enables us to forgive; yes, to remember, but to no longer be prisoner to the pain of that wrong. Forgiveness means we give up the right to hurt the person in retaliation. We let that go. We suspend the law of vengeance. And in John Ortberg's words, "when I forgive you, I set you free from the little prison I have placed in my mind for holding you captive."[48] We set them free, and we are set free! Sounds like a great deal to me!

Is there anyone today who needs to be transformed by your forgiveness? "Lord, is there?" Why not choose this day to forgive them, fully? Who knows? In doing so you may discover that you have set yourself free from the prison you put yourself in a long time ago. And you didn't even know that's where you've been living all this time.

"Committed Love"

Strongly associated with the Valentine's season are images of candlelight dinners, bouquets of roses, boxes of chocolates, romance, soft music, gushy outpourings of loving feelings, love-making and great expectations of being made to feel super-special. These are all good things, commendable and can strengthen marriage or dating relationships. (All except the love-making. That is only for the married, of course). In early February, the thoughts of many turn in the directions just outlined. These, however, are not the greatest examples of true love.

Years ago, a ministry friend named Bernie Smith, while speaking to a group of men, made this statement: "Love is not an ooey-gooey emotion. Love, is an act of the will." I've never forgotten that thought. Love is commitment. The best picture of love is not of a young couple holding hands over a candlelight dinner. It is of an elderly couple, frail, well-advanced in years, holding hands, totally relaxed in each other`s company, a testimony of the love that has endured through decades of challenges, hard times and shared memories. In spite of it all, they have remained committed and now share a deep bond and well of experiences no one else can even begin to comprehend. That is true love.

A commitment to love will be tested. Many fail the test. Unspoken marriage vows today often imply, "I will love you as long as I feel loving towards you. But if that goes away and we end up fighting and at odds it is far better that we separate so that our children will not grow up in a strained atmosphere of conflict, tension and oft-exchanged heated words." It sounds so noble. But it is pure rubbish – the rubbish of self-centered individuals committed only to the pursuit of their own personal happiness regardless of the consequences for others. What it teaches children is that if the going gets tough, you quit: that divorce is always a nearby back door. No, no. A thousand times no!

Committed love says, "Yes we are having disagreements. Yes, we may be in conflict from time to time. Yes, we may even express our feelings of disagreement inappropriately or loudly occasionally. But, bottom line, we will work out our differences. We will stay together, "for better or worse." We will grow together because we do love each other. We are committed. The lesson this teaches children is powerful. They learn that you do not quit when the going gets tough. You hang in there for the long-term results. One day you will be that elderly couple, comfortable with each other, tenderly holding hands, with a lifetime of unspoken memories between you, bonding you close. This, friends, is true Valentine's love. This is committed love. This is the impact it will have on children and others. I know, because I grew up with two parents just like this. I can remember the verbal fighting of their early years. But thankfully, I have the memories of their life together when in their eighties, still totally committed to each other in their own loving ways. Anchor your expectations of love in the solid reality of what is true love – an act of the will – commitment.

Adoption Love

One of the strongest of human drives is procreation. This is the powerful motivation and deep longing in a loving couple to create and raise children of their very own. God instilled this yearning as recorded in his Genesis 1:28 command to Adam and Eve: *"God blessed them; and God said to them, Be fruitful and multiply, and fill the earth, ..."* A couple who discover they cannot bear their own children due to infertility face a daunting challenge. According to an expert fertility specialist, every couple facing this must "resolve" their dilemma in one of several ways: adoption, in vitro fertilization, deciding not to pursue parenthood and reconciling themselves to that – these are some options they must choose from.

Through my last two years of Bible College, four years of graduate degree studies in seminary and well into our first pastorate my wife and I travelled this emotional journey. Eventually we chose adoption and began the trip down that road. The wait seemed long, yet was hope-filled. Then one day we received "the call." My wife took it at home, then called me at my church office. To this day I can picture myself standing by my desk, phone in hand, looking out the window while tears of joy streamed down my face as she informed me that our newborn baby girl was waiting for us to come and get her. Feelings of joy and love consumed me. I don't think we slept much that night. Early the next morning we made the three-hour drive to a nearby city where our daughter awaited us. Filled with excitement, we entered the social services office where we were directed to a nursery to wait. And then ... our precious twelve-day old Heidi was brought in and placed in our arms. I'm crying even now as I write, recalling the deep emotion of adopting this precious little baby as our very own child. These words are completely inadequate in conveying the joy and feelings the two of us felt in that little room with our little girl. Twelve years after our marriage we had finally become parents.

The formal, legal process of finalizing the adoption could not take place until after a mandatory six- month waiting period. But in the moment we first held her, she was already ours. Seven years later two more children also became ours through adoption. However, even then our family was not yet complete. Out first little baby girl has now turned 34! She and her loving husband Ryan have three precious daughters of their own, aged 9, 7 and 4 – our granddaughters. They are now all part of our family.

There is another family that is, in a far deeper way – if that is possible, built by adoption. It is one that I and many of you reading this have been brought into. This is God's very own eternal family. If I thought I loved my adopted family who bring feelings that stir my emotions at the deepest levels possible, this does not even begin to compare to the love and longings of our Creator God when he adopts us into his family. Do you realize how loved you are? *"In the same way, I tell you, there is rejoicing in the presence of the angels of God over one sinner who repents"* (Luke 15:10). This loving God longs for estranged humans, children of the god of this age, to come to him by trusting in his free gift of salvation provided through his son Jesus' death on the cross and resurrection from the dead. He longs to adopt us into his forever family. There is a family waiting for you. You can choose to join it today. Experience God's love!

ϕ

Chapter 10

ENCOURAGEMENT

Opportunity to Encourage

In the first church I pastored (so many years ago!), I came across a wonderful little verse. It meant so much that we printed it on all of our encouragement notes. It read: *"Anxious hearts are very heavy but a word of encouragement does wonders!"* (Proverbs 12:25, LB). Today I dug into what I call my "encouragement" file (the file where I've placed notes received across the years that have helped to 'keep me going' during many trying times). I came across a note written on one of those original forms. It contained heartfelt words from a dear lady expressing her gratitude to God for her church family and pastor. In her search for inner peace she had become involved in transcendental meditation. As a young pastor in my twenties God used me to have a part in helping her renounce her involvement in TM with its occultic influence, and in opening her life to salvation through the Prince of Peace, Jesus Christ, who filled her with His true peace! Later God used my wife and I in leading her senior-aged mother into a saving relationship with Jesus Christ. What a privilege. And what a chain of memories inspired by one little encouragement note!

Have you ever thought that your written words sent in a note could have a lasting impact like that decades later? How about a visit you made in somebody's home? Or even a phone call to listen and encourage that came at just the right moment? We don't know what impact such simple acts of caring have made in the lives of others, do we?

Do you remember when you prayed to receive Christ as your personal Savior? How did things go afterwards? Was there someone who came alongside to help you understand this new Christian life you had entered into, who answered your questions and mentored you along? Or were you left alone to sink or swim? Do you know of anyone who professed Christ as Savior, but then for lack of a mentor, fell away from their newfound faith, their roots never being given a chance to go down deep into Christ and produce fruit that would last? If only there had been someone just a little further along in their Christian walk, who would have spent some time with them, answering their questions and helping them to get grounded in Christ.

This all sounds pretty simple, doesn't it? It's not rocket science at all. It is ordinary people who know Jesus making time to do some simple things that could bring encouragement or direction that might have a life-long impact. Did you know this opportunity is available to you now? It is.

Who knows the difference your life might make in someone else's, leaving an impact for a long time to come? The power of one life touching one life multiplied many times over. Why not ask God to show you simple ways each day – today – to bring some simple encouragement into the life of someone you know?

Senior Supporters

The older you are the more encouraging you can be. After all, you've had more decades to trust the Lord and to have witnessed his faithfulness in your life. You can pass that on to others who are struggling. Let me back up this premise.

When I was 24 years of age my wife of three years and I left Canada and moved to a mid-western U.S. city for four years where I completed two Masters degrees. We knew only a handful of fellow Canadians who were also studying at the same seminary. We did not know where we would attend church but decided to visit all fifty-some churches in the metro area of our then denomination and take advantage of their special seminarian lunch invitations! It was a great plan, but at the second church we visited, we knew we had found our new spiritual home and looked no further. Within a few months of settling in, the Sunday School Superintendent, a dynamic senior in the congregation, asked if I would consider teaching the senior adult class in the church – the Bereans. "Who, me? I'm only 24." We met the group of loving folks in their 60's, 70's and 80's and fell in love with them. Teaching and fellowshipping with them became one of the most enriching experiences of our lives. The denomination provided an excellent adult curriculum. It was a joy to prepare the lesson each week and then to teach and grow with this great group of folks who, after all, were just a little older than us. What stories we could tell of their individual uniqueness and life histories.

Those seniors became our weekly encouragers throughout four challenging years of work and study. Introduced to an "eating out" culture, we were invited to join them every Sunday at one of the local buffets for lunch and for an evening snack after church. They vied to pick up the tab. This was a great blessing on our very limited student budget. A highlight of those years was the wedding of two of these seniors who met each other in the class, fell in love and shared a few short years together before he went home to be with the Lord. It was the most exciting wedding the church had witnessed!

In 1978 we finished our studies, said goodbye to our dear class and moved back to western Canada to our first pastorate. Louise Bird, a lady from the Bereans, regularly updated us on all their lives through notes and letters. However, their encouragement went beyond that. Fifteen years after we left them, Berean members got together in our honor and held a prayer meeting to pray for us. Can you believe it: 15 years later?! Little did they know we were in the midst of a very rough time having just finished our second pastorate of six years. What an encouragement was news of this meeting, their prayer and the picture they sent of the gathered group. Three years later they held a card shower for our 25th wedding anniversary. How delightful to receive warm greetings over twenty years after first meeting them. We were blessed. Most of those dear friends have gone home to heaven by now. Yet the legacy of their kind encouragement lives on in our lives.

It is never too late to reach back into our past to encourage, support and bless those who are younger and may need a lift. Who better than those of us who weathered life's storms and proved that God has seen us through?! Be a senior supporter!

A Family of Friends

I've been thinking about church lately. In my lifetime – I didn't set out to plan it this way but it is how God has led – I've been a part of fourteen churches spread across six denominations. I've been credentialed as a minister of the Gospel in four of them. This has given me a broad perspective of Christ's church. One of my roles was to teach church membership classes – which I did in four different denominational streams. That was been an education.

More importantly, I've been reminiscing about the impact of the church on my life personally. That's what matters for all of us. The Church – love it or dislike it – is the Body for whom Christ died. He told us the Church is His bride. He is preparing her for the day when he returns as the bridegroom to take His bride to live with Him forever. Christ loves the church. He laid down his life for the church. He is sanctifying His church. These are sobering thoughts whenever we are tempted to criticize 'the church.' For 'the church' is you ... and me ... His body, His building, His bride, His family.

The church as family is a powerful picture. Pastor Max Lucado observed: "You didn't pick me. I didn't pick you. You may not like me. I may not like you. But since God picked and likes us both, we are family." I confess there may be times when we get fed up with family dynamics. Yet, we remain, family. At other times, we are overwhelmed with the beauty of being family. I've come to love Lucado's description. "God offers you a family of friends and friends who are family – his church. When you transfer your trust into Christ, he not only pardons you; he places you in his family of friends.

"'Family' far and away outpaces any other biblical term to describe the church. 'Brothers' or 'brothers and sisters' appears a whopping 148 times between the book of Acts and the book of Revelation. God heals his family through his family. In the church, we use our gifts to love each other, honor one another, keep an eye on troublemakers, and carry each other's burdens."[49]

I shudder to think of what my life would have become without the family of the church surrounding me. Sure I've experienced moments of frustration, deep hurt and even rejection at the hands of the church – fellow members of the body. Yet, I love Christ's church for it has saved me time and again. I believe it was Augustine who said, if God is my Father, then the Church is my Mother. I now have friends in this family across multiple denominations and spread around the world. A growing host of them are in heaven awaiting my arrival to join them there one day.

Are you a committed member of Christ's church? Don't miss out on this life-saving privilege. Join what Robert Schuller called, "the corporate group of happy Holy Spirit-inspired Christians who allow themselves to be minds through which Christ can think, hearts through which Christ can love, hands through which Christ can help. In that sense, the church is the living body of Christ, helping hurting people in a local community."[50] Love His family. Be blessed by His family. Experience the support and encouragement of His family!

$$\phi$$

Chapter 11

MESSY LIFE

Seniors Behaving Badly

If you raised children earlier in your life do you recall how frustrating it was when they misbehaved? We adopted two children from orphanages in Romania. We later discovered they had special needs. Both were diagnosed as being ADHD among other issues. Their shenanigans, both at home and at school, would fill books, if described. As parents our patience was sorely tested, repeatedly. Not only that, we often had to deal with stressed teachers who had also been pushed to their limits by our son and daughter's actions. However, they were children and that is to be expected as part of the growing up, maturing experience. Once they reached adulthood, all lessons would have been learned and their behaviour would then be exemplary, right? Not necessarily so. But that's another story from our lives.

When we think of senior citizens – baby boomers and beyond – we may have this expectation of adults who are now characterized by mature behaviour. That belief could be a mistake. If you are on the internet and google "seniors behaving badly" you may be surprised at what comes up. Length of years lived does not automatically guarantee responsible behaviour! One reality of life is that as we age we tend to become more and more like what we are at present (unless we intentionally determine to change our patterns). Thus, people who have been kind, patient, loving and encouraging will tend to become even more like that as they get older. Those who have been impatient, critical, mean and cantankerous will become even meaner, more critical, more short-tempered and cantankerous as they get older. Those exemplifying such behaviors will become more and more a problem for themselves and others. Their relationships will undoubtedly become very messy.

The view of assisted-living or care homes may evidence such deeds. In fact, "Nearly 2,800 complaints are reported each year to the Department of Health and Services' Administration on Aging regarding fighting in long-term care facilities – and this is only the cases that are reported."[51] Homes like this may have their share of bullies and mean girls. Conflicts can arise over all kinds of slights and perceived offenses. Aggressive physical action may be taken against fellow residents or even care staff. The causes may lie in part because of mental health or medication issues. But often it is just plain immature, bad behavior – cantankerous middle-aged adults worsening as they get older. One does not need to live in a care home to experience this. It can happen in any neighborhood – even from adults who should be more grownup.

Another arena of senior misbehaviour is within families. Adult children caring for aging parents may enter a minefield of behavioral and relational blow-ups that can threaten to rob all joy from living. Sometimes these are simply the immature behaviors from child-rearing years carried on into the aging chapter of life. Long-rooted issues may need outside counseling and intervention before positive changes will occur. These are not easy to address but need to be faced for a better last season of life for all involved. There are resources that can be accessed, both online and in one's local community. Some helpful guidance may be found at the AgingCare.com website.[52]

For many older adults, the highlight of their week may be playing Bingo at their local community center. For others, relaxing pastimes may be much more extreme. For some older Brits, their favorite getaway is flying to Tenerife in the Canary Islands where they go to party hearty! One might witness there, pensioners binge-drinking and partying all night! A club manager observed that pensioners "can get quite raunchy after a few drinks!"[53] One club is nicknamed, "God's Waiting Room" because extreme partying behaviors may result in life-ending heart attacks that deliver individuals to the life hereafter. It is documented that some seniors, in their desire to escape from the U.K.'s miserable winters, may go overboard and squander their heating and grocery allowances in drinking and partying. Such lives seem to demonstrate the phrase *eat, drink, and be merry for tomorrow we die, which is a phrase that is an amalgamation of several Bible verses.*[54] It is often interpreted as meaning, to live one's life to the full for life is indeed short. However, in proper context, it is warning that such a lifestyle is short-sighted and not giving credence to the outcomes of such a selfish way to live. There are consequences of sin that will play out in one's own personhood, one's relationships and the testimony of one's life. It is okay to recreate, relax and renew but such a messy life as described above should be avoided at all costs.

Lost Zoomers

A couple of years ago I had opportunity to attend an exposition in our city featuring all things Zoomer – Zoomer being a description for a person born between 1946 and 1964 – putting an upbeat spin on those otherwise known as baby boomers. The focus was largely on services and resources available to those approaching or already in their senior years. I went with expectation of savouring the collective wisdom of the wisest of the wise, naively assuming that number of years lived will equal maturity, wisdom and a collective desire to impart a godly, inspiring legacy to following generations.

Imagine my surprise when I was instead greeted by personnel at booths promoting all things new-ageish! There were such items as Reiki – the laying on of hands to guide one's life force energy towards healing and health. Or how about tarot cards and psychic readings to help discover one's future. The benefits of acupuncture were touted: the penetration of the skin with needles stimulating specific acupuncture points to correct imbalances in the flow of qi (chi) through channels known as meridians – pure occultic philosophy. Then there was the booth soliciting support for medical marijuana: utilizing a mind-altering gateway drug containing over 483 known compounds creating psychoactive and mind-altering effects to somehow supposedly increase health! Dare I mention the free condoms that were being given away to fun-loving Zoomer singles?! The Buddhist, Hinduistic, free morality, occultic and demonic overtones were ubiquitous, openly espoused by the so-called wise of our society – our elders.

Upon reflection, I realized that I should not have been surprised. After all, are these not the hippy flower children of the '60's, who were then dressed in tye-died clothes, tripping out on acid and other psychedelic drugs while celebrating the cultural high point of Woodstock in 1969? We may be 45 years older but years lived does not automatically equal maturity. In fact, H. L. Mencken concluded: "The older I grow, the more I distrust the familiar doctrine that age brings wisdom."

There is no limit to the craziness of our world. Crazy living results in messy lives – very messy lives filled with sorrows, broken relationships and debilitating regrets. We see this demonstrated in beings all around us. Where is the needed wisdom to live life well? Just getting older doesn't guarantee it. How greatly is needed the example and influence of the lives of those who have learned to live well.

The apostle Paul said something similar in 1 Corinthians 3:19: *"For the wisdom of this world is foolishness in God's sight. As it is written: 'He catches the wise in their craftiness'."* The wisdom that worldly men esteem is foolishness with God.

Yet there is a godly wisdom that is to be desired and is needed. Elihu expressed it when he said in Job 32:7, *"I thought, 'Age should speak; advanced years should teach wisdom'."* Our world needs that wisdom. We who have lived longer can choose to leave a godly, inspiring legacy to following generations. Research shows that only about 1% of leaders are "legacy leaders" – those selfless individuals who have a burden to create a successful ministry that will last beyond their life-time. The wisdom for leaving such a legacy will come from those who base their lives on the solid truth of God's Word, not on the destructive teachings of new age and occult deception. Choose to live well and to be wise in God's eyes. Zoomers (as do all others) desperately need men and women of such godly wisdom. Become one.

Φ

Chapter 12

GOOD NEWS, SALVATION

It's Still GOOD News

Not long ago, world headlines decried the near collapse of the Italian economy, with that of Spain not far behind. The United States government failed to negotiate a one trillion-dollar budget reduction leaving America anxious about its fiscal future. Deficits and debt, balloon in countries around the world. Meanwhile, unemployment rates rose and "occupy" movements sprang up in cities globally to denounce the plight of the 99% who are not overly wealthy but only 'getting by.' Why, the daily news is downright depressing.

The Lord began whispering to my spirit about how I'd been responding to this steady barrage of not-at-all-good news. He reminded me that this is not the true picture of world affairs. That's not to say things are not bad in many ways and many places. They are. Then again, they always have been. Was it not Charles Dickens who so long ago penned the immortal words, "It was the best of times; it was the worst of times?"

The world was a rocky, unjust, dark and depressing place over two thousand years ago when into a black night an angelic messenger announced a transforming message. *"Do not be afraid, for behold, I bring you good tidings of great joy which will be to all people. For there is born to you this day in the City of David, a Savior who is Christ the Lord"* (Luke 2:10-11)! This was all part of a plan spanning the ages of the universe and announced centuries before through prophetic messengers. It was described later by the Messiah who came in the words, *"For God so loved the world that*

He gave his only begotten Son, that whoever believes in Him should not perish but have everlasting life. For God did not send His Son into the world to condemn the world, but that the world through Him might be saved" (John 3:16-17).

Did you read those words right through? I mean, when I come across familiar Bible verses I tend to scan past them, subconsciously thinking, I know all that. But read it again as if for the very first time. Talk about GOOD News?! This is what our dark world desperately needs to hear. The enemy of our souls knows it and does all he can to forbid the calling of it "Christ-mas" in the public square, referring instead to Happy Holidays. One year he raised up his servants to publicly oppose the distribution of Bibles to native children in northern Canada. He knows how dangerous this good news is to his destructive plans for mankind.

Perhaps my thoughts, and heart, were sent down this road by a visit with a dying woman. "God seems so far away," she said. "I haven't been able to feel Him these past three weeks. What's wrong?" she softly whispered. Joy sprang up as I realized I had good news to share with her. A prayer to affirm her salvation followed, then the reminder: *"He will never leave you nor forsake you"* (Hebrews 13:5). Never! Rest in His promise and not on your feelings." Peace and hope came over her countenance. Yes, it is still good news! It's the news we need to hear. It's the good news that can transform individuals for now and for eternity, even in the midst of the reports of so much bad news in the world in which we live.

Good News Received

The story of God's salvation may be over-familiar for many. There are various cultural icons making reference to it that are well-known. The flash of "John 3:16" signs on the TV cameras panning the crowds at various national football or baseball games is one. The image of Tim Tebow or other athletes well-known for their faith in God, kneeling in the end zone after scoring a touchdown is another. In our area, occasionally spotted are white lettering on blue background "Jesus Saves" or "Jesus is Lord" signs. Perhaps you've seen quirkily dressed individuals on street corners waving hard-to-miss signs declaring, "The End is Near," or "Jesus is Coming Soon?" We see this and they may or may not register on our consciousness, as it is easy to dismiss them as part of the North American social fabric that fades into the background. But there is a serious life-altering dimension to all this.

Jesus himself, the Son of God, said: *"Verily, verily, I say unto thee, Except a man be born again, he cannot see the kingdom of God"* (John 3:3, KJV). In a more up-to-date translation, it reads like this: "Jesus said, 'You're absolutely right. Take it from me: Unless a person is born from above, it's not possible to see what I'm pointing to – to God's kingdom'" (The Message). If I want to go to heaven when I die, and see God in his kingdom, I must be born again. Is that right? What does it mean to be "born again?" What if I'm not? These are critical questions. They affect our eternal destiny after our life here on earth is ended – which, by the way, could happen for any one of us at any time – even today. The issue then becomes, have you actually <u>received</u> this good news of salvation?!

The offer is for "whoever." That includes both you and me. No one is exempt from this invitation, no matter what kind of life they have lived up to now. We are invited. If we ignore the invitation or fail to respond we will not be part of God's eternal party. But if we do we will live with him forever in the place he has prepared for us. Anyone who trusts in him is acquitted; anyone who refuses to trust in him has long since been under the death sentence without knowing it. And why? Because of that person's failure to believe in the one-of-a-kind Son of God when introduced to him.[55] Have you put your trust in God and confessed your sins to him? Have you received his gift of forgiveness for the sin that separates you from him, and by faith and received his gift of eternal life? No one else can do this for you. Your parents' decision cannot count for you. We must each make this decision for ourselves.

When I was ten years of age, my mother had recently trusted in Christ to be her Savior. There was a definite change in her life – clear indicators that Christ had come into her life and was changing her. She also became passionate to share with others what God had done for her and to explain how they to could receive this gift of eternal life. Her children were among the first she talked to about this good news. One evening she told me what I explained in the above paragraphs. Then she asked me, "Do you want to pray to ask Christ to come into your heart?" I said, "Yes." We were sitting on her bed as we were having this conversation so she suggested I kneel there and repeat a prayer after her. I said a simple prayer confessing my sin to God. Even at that age I knew I was a sinner. I asked God to forgive me and to give me his free gift of eternal life. I waited to see what happened. Nothing. I was ready to give up. But Mom said, "No. Pray again. Tell him you really believe this and want him to come into your life. So, I did. I prayed one more time, this time putting my whole heart and faith into it. As I said "Amen" I opened my eyes and it seemed as if the whole world had changed. It seemed like everything was clean and white – washed brand new. I felt God had come into my heart and I knew he was now in me and that I belonged to him.

That personal sense of forgiveness has never changed, from that day to this. I know I am his and that, by faith, I will one day receive the reality of eternal life with him in heaven – a gift that is already mine by faith. The experience of assurance I received, I now know, was personal to me. The assurance of our salvation is unique to each person, for God knows what we each need. When he comes into our life we will have this "knowing" that he has indeed come in and will never leave. That was my experience of "receiving" God's good news gift of salvation. I close by asking you once more, have you received this gift for yourself? It is not yours until you do and without doing so, your state before God is to stand condemned. Invite him in right now.

φ

Chapter 13

CHRISTMAS AND OTHER SEASONS

Why Home for the Holidays?

The Christmas season is synonymous with "holidays." That's a good thing. But why is this pull so strong? For one, we can have so much fun when we get together with family and friends. One of my favourite stories comes from humorist, Robert Orben. "Some people,' he says, "are squeamish about raising their own holiday turkeys – but not me. Back in January we bought a turkey who became like a member of the family. We kept him in the house, fed him and took him for walks. But when the time came, there was no nonsense about it. We had him for Christmas dinner. He sat on my right."[56] I love that story!

Holidays are also good for us. They are akin to vacations. In fact, in Canada we call our vacations, holidays. Here are some interesting realities I learned about the beneficial effects of vacations that surely apply to holidays as well. "Researchers consistently find that vacations seem to do your heart good, reported the *Los Angeles Times*. The more you take them, the less likely you are to have a heart attack. For instance, findings, published in the *American Journal of Epidemiology* in 1992, reported that the least frequent vacationers (those who took no more than one vacation every six years) were at 50 per cent higher risk for a heart attack than the most frequent vacationers (those who took at least two vacations every year). Among stay-at-home spouses, the difference was higher: The least frequent vacationers faced about twice the risk of the most frequent vacationers."[57]

Holidays are both fun and beneficial. Here is an amazing thing. People, like me and maybe you too, will go through all kinds of travel distances and hassle to spend holiday time with those we love. Just think of the chaos of highways and airports at this season of the year. Why do we do this? We love to be with the ones we love, don't we? Picture the five-year-old granddaughter running down the walk to hurl herself into the arms of the Grandpa whose arrival she's been awaiting for hours. Or imagine the early morning coffee a young Mom has with her Mother when they get together on a holiday visit. Think about that moment when all are gathered around the table for a sumptuous feast, and are quietly, holding hands, praying a prayer of thanks for food and togetherness. Priceless! We love to be with those we love and will go to amazing lengths to get there, won't we?

Now, consider this. In Max Lucado's words, "So does God. ... How else do you explain what he did? Between him and us there was distance" – a heaven to earth separation! – "and he couldn't bear it ... so he did something about it. 'He gave up his place with God and made himself nothing' (Philippians 2:7)."[58] Incredible! You want to spend holidays with your loved ones for good reasons. Yet, how incredibly more God wants to be with you! Enjoy His Presence and being with your loved ones during the next season. Happy Holidays!

A Christmas Blessing

"It's the most wonderful time of the year..." With those words of a popular song we launch into the Christmas season. In many ways, it is a wonderful time of the year. For some though, it is a very difficult time. It is a season of opportunity and celebration. It may also be a season of nostalgia or sadness. What will this next Christmas be for you?

One common experience for many will be that of coming together with family or others in special gatherings. These offer occasions for parents and grandparents to impart a blessing to those around them.

In their book, *The Blessing*, Gary Smalley and John Trent outlined the five components of a "family blessing" in this way:

"A family blessing begins with *meaningful touching*. It continues with *a spoken message of high value*, a message that pictures a *special future* for the individual being blessed, and one that is based on an *active commitment* to see the blessing come to pass."59

In brief moments of connecting we may seize chances to make a profound impact on those we love. Meaningful touches. Spoken messages verbalizing what is in our hearts. Attaching high value to the person or persons we are blessing. Picturing a special future for the one we are blessing and telling them what we see. All of this followed by actively committing ourselves to fulfill the blessings we impart.

Chuck Stecker, a speaker at a CASA Conference in Atlanta I once attended, sensitized me to the tragedy in the church of having failed to receive and give blessings to succeeding generations (Read *Men of Honor, Women of Virtue*). This has impacted those in the senior years, not only the younger generation. I have much to learn about and mull over in terms of how we might make a difference to this present reality. But for now, it strikes me that the Christmas season could be a time in which we look for moments when we could bless those we care about. Our touch, our word, our blessing, the future picture we paint for someone, the commitment we make to them could turn around someone's destiny. None of us are too old or too young to do that.

An esteemed clergyman in England told J. Wallace Hamilton, "The turning point in my life came when I was seventeen years old. I was called the black sheep in my family. We were always fighting each other. One night, my mother, my father, my brother and sister kept picking on me until I couldn't stand it anymore. I jumped up and cried, 'I am leaving. I'm getting out of here.' I ran up the stairs, and in the darkened hallway, I suddenly ran into my grandmother. She had been listening to it all ... the diatribes, the accusations, the vilifications. She just stood there, put her hand on my shoulder, and, with tears in her eyes, said five words that changed my life forever: 'John, I believe in you.'"[60]

This is the nature of the blessings we can pass on this Christmas season. Let's look for opportunities to do so. Who knows the lifetime of difference it might make for the one we bless?!

An African's Christmas

It was Christmas 1968. Having finished my first semester at college 350 miles away from home, I looked forward to returning to the family farm for the holidays. However, I had an unusual request for my parents. Could I bring a college friend home with me? Unusual why, you ask? This friend was from Africa. He was new to snow, Canadian Christmases and farms! My folk's response was an immediate "yes!" The day after classes ended, Aaron and I set out on the seven-hour journey in my old 1952 Chevy. It was an eventful ride over snow-packed to center-bare roads. In the early darkness, we arrived safely home. Warm hugs abounded for all.

That Christmas was memorable primarily due to Aaron's elated response to ... everything! New falling snow brought exclamations of glee! Meeting, petting, feeding and hanging around all the barn animals brought oohs and aahs of joy. Inclusion in our family meals and Christmas Day celebrations opened his eyes wide with pleasure. Laughter filled the air. Wonder never seemed far from his countenance. Though half a world away from his family and most of all, his dear fiancé, Elizabeth, he seemed elated to share our simple farm Christmas and family experience. His loneliness was lifted. His constant delight is the memory that remains with me across these many years.

Aaron was sent by his country to complete a two-year Geology Technician program. On his completion, he returned to Swaziland to work in that field for his government. Through mutual connections we subsequently learned that he did marry his dear Elizabeth, had a family with her and worked in geological research for many years. He also served faithfully in the church denomination which had first drawn us together. Though we never heard directly from him again, we learned he was doing well.

The Bible commands: *Don't forget to show hospitality to strangers, for some who have done this have entertained angels without realizing it!* (Hebrews 13:2, NLT). To my simple way of thinking, I wonder how much angels really need to be entertained by us since they continually come back and forth from the very presence of God? What could possibly be greater than that for them? But oh, how very much lonely, hurting, or broken people may need loving hospitality. Who knows what an unselfish opening of our homes and our hearts might mean for their healing and restoration, or to just remind them they are not alone and that someone cares? People who may think God does not even know them, let alone care about them, may be brought into the very presence of God by common folks like us. But here's the real kicker. In opening ourselves up to them, we may discover a joy and a blessing that lasts and encourages us for a lifetime! That's what Aaron's visit did for our family. He was not the only one who benefitted from that Christmas together.

Let's look around this next Christmas season. Let's ask God to open our eyes. Who knows who he may prompt us to invite into our spaces and how that may result in a mutually-shared lifetime joy?!

Delightful Gift Giving!

It was the cutest little train. With cardboard trestles painted to look like stonework, the track could be laid out in a figure eight pattern allowing the train to go over and under itself. We played with that Christmas gift by the hour when we were little children. It was exactly what we wanted. How did our parents know that three little boys would have so much fun with this gift?! Between uses we carefully stored the set in an empty dresser drawer. This diligence later prompted our Grandmother to entrust us with an even larger Lionel train set she owned. Wow! Blessing added to unexpected blessing.

This memory prompts me to think of an even greater and far more significant gift that was given to me when I was a child of ten. This was a gift I've enjoyed not only for my whole life here on earth, but will continue to relish for eternity. It is the gift of God's salvation. By it I was forgiven of all my sin that would have separated me from God forever, and I was brought into a relationship with Him that continues to this very day. Double Wow! His presence continues to transform everything about me on a daily basis. How could I have known this was just what I needed?!

December is the month in which we commemorate the event that made this gift possible. Our parents loved their little boys enough to give them a costly gift that would bring them great delight. To a far greater degree, Father God loved us so much he gave us His most costly gift – His one and only Son. He gave us Jesus knowing this was the gift we needed most. More than great delight, it would bring us into a never-ending relationship with Him. So He gave. Salvation.

My wife and I have three young adult children (and three precious granddaughters). Every Christmas we delight to give them special gifts. In fact, my wife Bev always has some in hand months in advance! That's what love does. Love moves us to give. One of the amazing things about God's love is that He just keeps on giving and giving. For instance, when faced with insurmountable problems or setbacks, we are given the option of turning everything over to Him in prayer, while giving thanks for the unexpected challenge before us. In turn, he gives us the incomprehensible gift of supernatural peace of mind and heart that quiets us as we go through the life-altering situation (Philippians 4:6-7). Gift upon gift! Have you experienced God's love lately? Have you thanked Him for the delight He continues to bring into your life – every day in so many ways? This month let's do that more than ever before. Yes, let's keep on giving in love. But let's also take notice of all He is giving to us – just what we needed when we didn't even know we did – and in the process bringing us such great delight. "Thank you, Lord. It was just what I wanted!"

Christmas Nostalgia

Is there anything more nostalgic than decorating your home for Christmas?! With Christmas carols playing in the background and familiar tree ornaments waiting to be placed carefully on the tree, memories come flooding in. Nostalgia is "a sentimental longing or wistful affection for the past, typically for a period or place with happy personal associations." The "Bah, humbug!", "I can't believe another whole year has gone by," and "What on earth are we going to give _____ as a gift this year?" comments fade into the background as pleasant past memories nudge their way to the foreground. An angel purchased by this young couple over 45 years ago, is gently placed at the peak of the tree. The halo of lights surrounding her have been replaced once, but other than for that, she has survived relatively unscathed, still in her original, though slightly tattered, box. Yet in the moment she is set in place, scenes of 45 years surrounding her come flooding in. A couple alone, parents (now gone) visiting, three children growing up year by year, turkey dinners enjoyed by family and friends at the nearby table, the tree set up in several homes in various cities, multiple lovingly chosen gifts, given and received, and now grandchildren taking their part in the ongoing, steadily unfolding Christmas story in our home – how special for us are these moments of recall! Have you felt it?

Memories. At the same time, having reached the early senior years, another question comes to mind. How many more of these Christmases will we be privileged to experience before reaching the end of our earthly days? Part of the nostalgia comes from thoughts of parents and other loved ones who are no longer with us. They were our bedrock: the ones we could always count on to be here. But they have finished their earthly journey. When will our turn come? This is a reality to be faced. Life is passing quickly. We can hardly believe the number of years that have gone. They went by so fast! This is a strong encouragement to make the most of these moments. They are a gift for which to give thanks. I for one am deeply grateful for every single Christmas season I've been privileged to live through.

As I contemplate my unknown number of years remaining I'm deeply grateful to know I am prepared for what is to come. The facts of the Jesus event – what Christmas is all about, have made it possible for me to prepare. I was fully aware that inside me, as inside every single person, is a God-shaped hole that only God can fill. You know what I'm referring to, don't you? It's that feeling of something missing deep inside: an emptiness, a nostalgic longing for something more. That gnawing 'deep calling to deep,' are our spiritual hunger pangs. We know we are incomplete; that something is missing. Oh, we'll seldom admit this to anyone else. Yet, it is there. For all of us. To paraphrase an early Church Father, we are made for God and our hearts are restless until we find ourselves in him.

Why this emptiness? Whether we want to accept it or not, the truth is, we are separated from God, both by the sinfulness of the general human condition and by the sins we've committed in our own lives. God does not naturally live and reign inside us. We live apart from him. Thus, the void, the longing. God does not want us to remain like this. He loves us too much. That is the Christmas story. He loved us so much he gave us his one and only Son, who came as the baby Jesus, fully man, yet fully God. Then in his death and resurrection he bore the penalty of all the sins that kept us away from God, conquered the last great enemy, death, and made it possible for that empty hole in each of us to be filled by God himself, God coming to live inside of us. Have you invited him to live in and rule your life? Once you do, the emptiness ends. In its place is not only a new assurance that God has filled the space made for him but also a new awareness that we will live eternally with him after we die. This eternal life begins in us right now.

This leads to a new sense of nostalgia – a wishful longing for something yet to come. It's the final home for which we sense we were ultimately made. It's a sentimental yearning, not for what is past, but for what is to come. The advent season of Christmas, points us to the Savior who came as a baby in a manger (past), who comes to us now as we open our hearts and lives to him (present), and who is coming again one day to take us home to heaven to live with him forever (future). Nostalgia: backwards and forwards! Are you experiencing the full nostalgia of Christmas this season, both past and future?

The Time of Singing Birds

It had been a brutal winter for much of North America with record snowfalls burying vast tracts of landscape. In contrast, for those on the Southwest Coast of British Columbia and in the Pacific Northwest it had been mild with virtually no snow that winter season. And now, flowers were pushing their way up through the warming earth, trees were budding and we were awakened by the wonderful sound of singing birds. I am reminded of that verse in Song of Songs 2:12: *The flowers are springing up, and the time of singing birds has come … (NLT).* In southern California folks are encouraged each spring, when the swallows return to San Juan Capistrano. Around St. Joseph's Day (March 19) their songs fill the old Spanish Mission. I walked those grounds one spring day and was cheered by their twittering presence everywhere.

These spring indicators remind us that no matter how dark the season that we've been through, there comes a time for new beginnings, fresh starts and inner urges to get up, get out and be doing. Hope arises once more. The farm I grew up on lay in the snow belt of southern Ontario. One time we were snowed in and could not get out to school for an entire week. As kids, we thought it was wonderful! Winters were long and harsh. But, they ended. The snow melted and the urge to plant new crops filled each farmer's heart afresh. It was so good to get back on the land, working it, preparing it and sowing fresh seed in readiness for a new harvest in fall. There is an encouraging, God-ordained rhythm to life.

Are you despairing of that rhythm? Has hope fled? Do you feel locked in an emotional never-land of unbroken winter? Is depression or discouragement stifling your heart like a smothering blanket of cold snow? The circumstances of life can do that to us: unexpected reversals; unwanted tragedies; unrelenting pressures; unyielding burdens. We may despair that it will never end. Take heart my friends: *the time for the singing of the birds will come!* God has ordained it. It's built into the economy of His universe.

Hang on a little longer. You are not forgotten, not forsaken. He hears the silent, longing cry of your aching heart.

When I was fifteen, my six-year-old sister Janie died after a long, two-year battle with leukemia. Our world ended on that cold October day in 1965. We went through the motions and laid her little body to rest in that lonely country cemetery. Broken-hearted, my family struggled to carry on with life. But the winter passed. Spring came once more. And in a real sense life did continue. Now over fifty years of living have ensued. God has proven faithful through a multitude of other life challenges since that sad day. I am reminded that His mercies, His compassions, are new ever morning. Great is His faithfulness. Therefore, I will hope in Him (Lamentations 3:22-24). He does not forsake us. He will not forsake you.

Do you hear it? The twittering? The chirping? The time for the singing of the birds will come. Watch for the new flowers to spring up in your life circumstances. They will push their way to the surface. The song will return. God does love you. You are not alone. Watch for Him. He is near.

July Memories

"There is a time for everything, and a season for every activity under heaven" (Ecclesiastes 3:1). The coming of summer brings a rhythm of its own unlike the other seasons of the year. Looking back across more than six decades brings a flood of memories from past Julys. As a teenager, it meant weeks of haying season on the family farm in hot, humid southern Ontario. Working alongside our Dad we three sons spent hours each day mowing, baling and then hauling bales by the wagon load to the barn, then loading them onto the elevator which took them up into the loft where we piled them in carefully arranged mows. The supply of hay would see our livestock through the long months of fall and winter. It was back-breaking, sweaty work that built up our muscles while exhausting us by day's end.

Later on, July became synonymous with Scout Camp at Haliburton Scout Reserve and the opportunity to learn new outdoor skills and form new friendships. Water sports, night games and the grueling three day 50-mile long canoe trip with its tough portages, added entirely new dimensions to life.

One particular July in 1971 is especially memorable, for on its tenth day I met my beautiful bride at the altar of the Alliance Church in Thunder Bay, Ontario. We exchanged vows and began what now adds up to a 46-year journey of married life together. That was the best July ever!

During the college and seminary period of early marriage, July meant summer employment working in the trucking industry, driving intercity passenger buses and building homes in the US Midwest. All of these were entirely new and varied life experiences. With the commencement of a lifetime of pastoral ministry in 1978, July brought Vacation Bible School, summer camps and family vacation memories spread across two provinces and three cities of Canada. July during our nine years in Calgary was synonymous with our annual Calgary Stampede Pancake Breakfast and outdoor

Western Service on the lot beside our church. What a variety of personalities that brought into our lives – both visitors and entertainers!

At this present stage of life July is appreciated for a slightly slowing pace of church life from the usual hectic full-on schedule of the church year. If possible, it means some significant time away camping or recreating in other ways during annual vacation times. This summer season includes memories of scenes from British Columbia to Northwestern Ontario, two visits to Barkerville and Prince George, camping in the Kootenays and our most favourite of all, camping for a week each summer at Swan Lake near Vernon with our little granddaughters. So special!

Solomon closed his book with this reality: *Life, lovely while it lasts, is soon over. Life as we know it, precious and beautiful, ends. The body is put back in the same ground it came from. The spirit returns to God, who first breathed it.* (Ecclesiastes 12:6-7, *The Message*). Our Father, who is faithful in every season of life, intends for us to experience this one to the full. Soon enough our Julys will end and we'll then be with Him forever. Enjoy life here now and make the very most of every summer!

Simply Thankful

October is the month equated with leaves changing colour, then letting go their hold on life as fall sets in. In Canada, this month is also synonymous with thanksgiving. Growing up on a farm in rural Ontario, this made perfect sense. October marked the completion of crops being harvested and gratitude for another year's bounty. On the second Sunday of the month, displays at the front of the church were filled with vegetables, fruits of all kinds, perhaps a pie or two, not to mention the requisite canned goods and preserves. These were destined for the needy in our midst. That was the pastor and his family! Thanksgiving rolls around every year. But how do we keep it fresh and meaningful?

This is a special challenge with the passing of years. Losses mount and disappointment, even bitterness, can easily be allowed to take up residence. Deaths of dear ones may bring loneliness and grief. Setbacks, hardships, unfilled expectations or crashed hopes may converge to crush hope. "Thankful? For what?" we may think. May I suggest, for all the simple things, the take-for-granted things which may be overlooked. Begin with life. Life is a gift: that's why it's called, the "present". Believing we are here for a reason and that God has a purpose for which he will use us every single day (we are and He does!), gives meaning. "Thank you God for life. Use me today."

What about those tough things you had to endure? Josh McDowell once had a long discussion with God about the imperfect, often terrible parents he had been given. He wrestled with God (it's okay to do that, you know) about this hard reality. Then the Lord whispered to him: "Josh, do you like who you are today and what you are doing?" Josh had to honestly affirm that he did. Then the Lord asked: "What do you think I used to make you what you are?" That shook him. His parents were indeed part of God's shaping plan! Often the things we despised, rejected or despaired over were God's building blocks in making us. A profound truth learned in my past reminds me to "look at what you have left, not at what you have lost." Thank you again God.

I came across a cute scenario recently. This note was left beside an empty glass. "While you, the Pessimist (glass half empty) and you, the Optimist (glass half full) were busy arguing, I drank the water." Signed, the Opportunist! Thank you, God ... for a fresh drink of water! New opportunities! Don't get bogged down. Look for the them. There are so many serendipities in life. Notice them. As we do, don't overlook the obvious. One day recently, during a very routine day, I was suddenly overwhelmed with gratitude for the gift from God to me of my dear wife. I realized I would never have become what I have without her friendship and love these 47 plus years I have known her. Although easily taken for granted, in those moments I was moved to fervent prayer of gratitude for this precious gift of God to me and prompted to pray much blessing over her as she slept. Thank you, Lord. What do you have, to be simply thankful for this month? Give thanks!

Discontent, or Thanksgiving?

The Thanksgiving season would soon be upon us here in Canada. Yet for some reason I found the title of one of John Steinbeck's novels running through my head. *The Winter of our Discontent* was written in 1961 and was perhaps his best novel. Set in a New England town, it tells the story of Ethan Allen Hawley, a Harvard grad from a wealthy family who had lost their capital during WWII through a serious of bad business ventures. Now, working as a clerk in the grocery store he had once owned, it chronicles the discontent of he and his wife Mary with their new lot in life, and his downward spiral in integrity and compromise to do whatever it took to try to regain their lost material status. In a sense, it depicted the broader struggle in society to choose pursuit of affluence and riches, no matter what the cost to morality or personal character, thus weakening the strength of a culture.

This is a personal battle ever before each of us. In the face of lack and lesser (as compared to the mythical next-door Joneses) do we wallow in discontent, or do we instead choose to be grateful for what we do have?

In direct contrast to Ethan Hawley's life approach is that reflected in the lyrics of the worship song Don Moen made famous in 1986:

> *"Give thanks with a grateful heart, Give thanks to the Holy One*
>
> *Give thanks because He's given Jesus Christ, His Son.*
>
> *And now let the weak say, 'I am strong'*
>
> *Let the poor say, 'I am rich*
>
> *because of what the Lord has done for us.'"*[61]

Focus on lack and be discontented, or focus on who we are and what we have in Christ and be thankful? How many times a day do we each face this very choice?

I grew up on a 100-acre mixed farm in southern Ontario, Canada, where life was always a struggle. I don't think the farm books ever showed a year-end profit balance in all those years of operation. I have memories of my father going to the bank (and seeming to be put through the wringer by bank authorities) to try to borrow money to drill a new well or to buy a new tractor when the old one had finally packed it in. There was seldom a little extra money to send along with me to high school so I could buy snacks or the occasional meal in the school cafeteria. I took a brown-bag lunch. My clothes, though I cared for them well, were never in style and were often hand-me-downs. I could go on with instances of my youthful experiences of "lack." We could have been very discontented.

Yet what I remember was always having enough: food to eat, clothes to wear, a home to live in, warm beds to sleep in and special treats and experiences that made life rich. Church attendance and faith in God laid a foundation of family thankfulness that permeated our home. Trials and tribulations were many – and frequent – but gratitude was the de facto standard reflected in our parents' lives and caught by we, their five children. When that Christian faith came alive as one-by-one we discovered Jesus Christ as our personal Savior, the thanksgiving quotient increased exponentially.

Are you feeling weak? Instead say, "I am strong." Feeling poor? Say, "I am rich – because of what Christ has done for me." Please don't wallow in discontent. Be grateful. Begin to live! It is your choice. Choose well. And oh, "Happy Thanksgiving!"

ϕ

Chapter 14

TRANSITIONS, ENDINGS, EXITS

Brexit and Other Exits

In June 2016, by a narrow margin (52%), the people of the United Kingdom (Britain) voted to leave the European Union. It was nicknamed, Brexit. Immediately forecasts proliferated regarding all kinds of dastardly harm that would befall this country and the world as a consequence of this exit. That is not an uncommon reaction. Exits are difficult. Personally, I've gone through five exits from churches where I had pastored. The results of these leavings proved to be mixed, but at the time there was a measure of anxiety about what the consequences of going might be. "Exit" is both a noun (a way out, the act of going out or leaving a place) and a verb (to go out or leave a place; depart, withdraw, retreat). Have you had any difficult exits in your life?

Exits, whether voluntary or forced, can be challenging. Yet, they are a part of everyone's life sooner or later, no matter how hard we may try to play it safe and avoid them. The whole thing about life that doesn't change – is that life constantly changes! Rather than dreading the changes brought about by exits, we must learn to accept that they will come, and find a philosophy, an approach that will ground us and guide us for when those exit doors appear in our lives. Exits may take many shapes: leaving the security of the parental home as a teenager or young adult to begin life on one's own; the end of singleness to enter the life of marriage; entering the years of parenthood; the empty nest as the last child leaves home, leaving you behind; exiting a job or position for a new one or, transitioning into unemployment; leaving the work force to move into retirement; the end of a relationship, or a marriage; and then the final exit – the conclusion of our earthly journey through death and entrance into what is next. Do these examples of exits stir up emotions of loss, sadness, fear, anxiety, anger, depression, or perhaps, excitement, joy or anticipation?

Have you found a formula, a foundation that prepares you for such exits so that you know you will remain at peace and be confident in the midst of such storms of uncertainty? The Psalmist David of Old Testament fame had done so. In Psalm 46 he spoke of the end of the earth (that's a major exit!), natural calamities of earthquakes and hurricanes (which often cause loss of houses, jobs and everything else that may be a consequence), and the fallout of wars and military regimes with the ends they bring to many lives. He mentions the worst exits possible. Then he talks about God as his refuge; God being his strength; God who is his ever-present help in the midst of troublesome exits. He describes a beautiful place of calm serenity where God is in complete control – the holy place where God dwells. He states that the presence of and relationship with this God can be our fortress (place of protection) for he is with us. Does this sound too good to be true, to help you in the midst of your life exits? I assure you, it is real. He extends to us an invitation: *"Be still and know that I am God; ... the Lord Almighty is with us; the God of Jacob is our fortress"* (vs. 10-11).

Are you facing some fear-inspiring transitions in your life? Relax. Focus. Deliberately put your trust in God. He is in ultimate control. You can trust Him. He will bring you safely through to the other side of your exit experiences. I know, because He has for me.

13:8, 84, 16 & Change

First, 13:8, as in Hebrews 13:8 – *"Jesus Christ is the same yesterday and today and forever."* The hymn writer wrote long ago, "Change and decay in all around I see. O Thou who changest not, abide with me."

Change. It is an inevitable part of life. In fact, the only thing about life that doesn't change – is that life is constantly changing! Yet, we value homeostasis so much we tend to strongly resist change. Homeostasis is the natural tendency of an organism to maintain a stable, constant inner condition. When it comes to God, that is indeed acceptable; actually, it's desirable. We need to know that God, who has said from the beginning that He loves His highest creation, mankind, still loves us now just the same. We need to know that Creator God who was all powerful and all knowing when He created the universe, is still omnipotent and omniscient today. We must know that God does not change. We need to know that grace and forgiveness remains his dominant attitude toward us.

But what about us? What about our lives? We live in constant tension (not always a bad thing, by the way). On one hand, we desire that things constantly remain the same – that homeostasis exists in and around us. On the other hand, our experience has shown that there is little growth and improvement in life without change. Where do we come out on this tension? Keep things the same, or change?

Howard Hendricks[62] points out that 84% of the people in any church are ripe for change. They long to see growth, personally and in their church. There is no growth without change. Although it may initially be uncomfortable, they are ready for change. The flip side is that 16% of the people in any church (perhaps confusing themselves with God?!) will NEVER change! That's rather sad, though unfortunately, true. The tragedy comes when pastors or leaders listen only to the 16%, give up and quit trying to lead. That's

140

tragic. The real ministry of the church takes place when leaders concentrate their energies on the 84% who are ready to change and better, are willing to get on board and help make positive changes happen.

So, here's the issue: 13:8, 16, or 84? Which best describes me? You? And if it's 16, here's really good news. We CAN change! When change is successful we look back at it and call it growth!

Real Grief

On February 6, 2006, my Father died. On March 1, 2012, my Mother died. I am now an orphan. True, that well into my sixth decade of life, this is not at all a remarkable occurrence in life stages. Yet, it is personally moving. There is something sobering about becoming the family's new patriarch (as the oldest child) while still grappling with the loss of one's parents.

Death seems so final. It is, as the apostle Paul observed, the last great enemy. Everything changes irreversibly with the death of a loved one. The grieving of what has been lost takes many forms and twists along the ensuing journey. Feelings of sadness, melancholy, nostalgia or pain may be triggered at any moment by multiple prompts in daily life. A simple event brings back a memory of the deceased loved one and emotions suddenly flood in. Tears well up. One is suddenly struggling to pull oneself together in order to carry on with present duties. Such is the process of grieving.

A huge help in this journey is a ministry called *GriefShare* – your journey from mourning to joy – which is available at locations around North America. It has hugely helped many in walking through their grief and is a highly-recommended resource for all, no matter when your loss may have occurred.[63] Facing loss, understanding it, discussing it can result in new levels of acceptance, healing and ability to move on with life. Otherwise, one can easily become stuck, unable to get beyond the loss.

Grief results anytime and every time we lose something significant to us. Whether it is a much-prized car that got obliterated in an accident, a cherished possession that was stolen, a dear pet that died or a precious loved one who passed on, we will go through the grief process. The intensity of the grieving will vary depending on the significance of the loss. We'll grieve the death of a loved one far more than the loss of the car! However, we will go through the same process. Understanding this fact may help explain those flashes of anger or feelings of sadness one may encounter. To be able to say to oneself, "I am grieving a loss and these feelings I'm having are natural and to be expected," can put them in perspective and keep them from having a far worse impact upon us. From there we can move on to tell ourselves that, "I will eventually get beyond this and one day life will resume as normal – granted, a new normal – once more. This is not the end of my world." With that, hope may spring anew.

Are you grieving? Get support. Enroll in a *GriefShare* session. Shed some tears – lots of them as needed, whether you are a woman or a man! Pour out your heart to God – even if it is expressions of extreme anger. God is big enough; He can take it. Besides, He already knows what you are feeling about Him anyway! Tell him. Then tell yourself, "There is life beyond this loss and one day I will be able to go on with life once again." Allow hope to be born in you once more. He is our God of all comfort and of green hope! Invite Him to walk with you through your days of loss. I am.

In Loving Memory

"In Loving Memory." Read those words and we immediately think of a beloved relative or friend, deeply cherished, who is now no longer with us here on earth. Pause for a moment and our minds and hearts will be filled with nostalgic memories surrounding that person. Think a little longer and, for those of the baby boom generation at least, the haunting voice of Barbra Streisand may echo in our minds singing the words: "Memories, May be beautiful and yet, What's too painful to remember, We simply choose to forget. So it's the laughter, We will remember, Whenever we remember, The way we were."[64]

November is the month of Remembrance as well as the precursor to the season (Christmas) that triggers a plethora of memories. November 11th all across Canada, on the eleventh day at the eleventh hour the nation pauses to remember those who laid down their lives in wars long past, and current, to protect the freedoms we have come to cherish in this great land of ours. For a few moments each year, we remember and pay tribute to those heroes, long gone, whose sacrifice impacts us to this very day. To you we say, "Thank you."

At Remembrance Day, we are only two months away from celebrating the annual Christmas holiday once again. Few holiday celebrations bring as much joy as this. However, for many, few may bring as much pain. Memories of loved ones who were once absolutely integral to the joy of the festivities, but now absent through death, may leave us despondent, struggling to continue. Many wonder, "How can I go on?" As the season approaches the dread increases. "How can I survive another holiday filled with so many memories of happier times, in face of the harsh reality that my loved one is missing?" How indeed?

A program called *GriefShare*, offers an invaluable seasonal seminar experience entitled, "Surviving the Holidays." It is filled with ideas, hints, insights and hope-filled approaches to develop a realistic, helpful plan to better handle the memories and to build new, better ones for future going-forward. Find out where this is offered near you and take advantage of this helpful, healing experience.[65]

However, right now, as a daily experience there is deep, deep help for the memories that burn, churn and ultimately depress. It's found in a short, simple verse from the Bible. *"Casting all your cares upon Him, for He cares for you"* (1 Peter 5:7). Jesus knows. He hears. He does care. Peter knew Jesus first-hand. Peter knew Jesus would do this for us so he wrote it down. Jesus will help you carry your load of memory and pain. Talk to him about whatever is troubling you right now, just as you would an intimate friend across the table over a cup of coffee. Unload. Let go. He'll carry your care for you.

Remembering. Dad, Father, Mom, Janie, Aunt Ethel, Rick, Joanell, Mel … so many, many dear ones … all once a vital part of my life and now gone. But they are in good hands. I long ago turned them over to Jesus and He is taking wonderful care of them all! I choose to remember the laughter and the way we were. For these memories too I simply say, "Thank you."

φ

Chapter 15

DEATH, ETERNITY

Life Is Short: Live With Care

We once had a speaker at a seniors' gathering who presented a workshop on "Death Matters" – helpful information we should all have about what goes on behind the scenes and what needs to be taken care of in the event of the death of a loved one. Death: not something we normally want to think about. When young, we know we'll live forever and never die! If we do live to reach the second half of life a semblance of reality crowds in with niggling reminders that our life here is limited and will one day come to an end (unless the Lord returns first). Such wispy thoughts are usually accompanied with impressions of unbelief at how quickly life has flown by. The further along we journey in the second half of life, the stronger grows the certainty that our days are indeed numbered and will soon come to a close. How do we live meaningfully in view of this growing awareness? Various approaches can be taken.

Some will do all they can to smother these reminders with noise, activity and fun: "Eat, drink and be merry for tomorrow we die." For them the highest goal is "to be happy." How foolish, our Lord said, for we must all soon face judgment for the deeds we did in the body. We will give an account. It is fitting for us to live well.

At the other extreme is the goal expressed by the Apostle Paul as he neared the end of his life. *"6For I am already being poured out like a drink offering, and the time has come for my departure. 7I have fought the good fight, I have finished the race, I have kept the faith. 8Now there is in store for me the crown of righteousness, which the Lord, the righteous Judge, will award to* me on that day—and not only to me, but also to all who have longed for his appearing" (2 Timothy 4). This approach says, "I must live my life well before God for he has a crown he wants to present to me when I give an account. The reward will be accompanied by His words, 'Well done, good and faithful servant.'" Every day we can choose to live life with a view toward this reality.

In between these extremes are those negative, critical persons who seem to respond to every life situation with a shrug that in effect says, "That's the way I am. That's my personality. There's nothing I can do about things. Life always treats me badly. I always get a raw deal." If that's your usual response I have two words for you: "Stop it!" Choose life, not death. You do have a choice. If you have been a chronically negative person whose first response to every change and challenge has been "no way," "it's impossible," or "I can't," stop it! It's not too late to change. By God's help, and in fulfillment of His will for your life, you can become a positive, hope-filled person by the renewal of your mind – be "*a fresh new person in all you do and think*" (Romans 12:1,2)!

Yes, our time on earth is limited, but we can choose to live it well. We may not receive a Lifetime Achievement Grammy award as did gospel singer, George Beverly Shea, at age 102! But we can receive one greater than that: Christ's "well done." Now that's worth living for.

Graduation, then What?

The month of June brings association with many nostalgic memories. Not the least of those was school year-end and graduations: school's out! The long summer stretched ahead. Some remember it as a time for freedom: "No more pencils, no more books; no more teachers' dirty looks!" Goodbye homework and assignments; hello lazy days, play and fun – which, if we are honest about our memories, soon morphed into boredom. "There's nothing to do around here!" But that came later. The initial feelings were good.

As we grew up, of course, reality set in. Charles Sykes, author of "Dumbing Down Our Kids," shared some of the humorous lessons we learned about life. See if you confirm these from your own experience.

"Life is not fair. Get used to it."

"The world won't care about your self-esteem. It will expect you to accomplish something before you feel good about yourself."

"Sorry, you won't make $80,000 a year right out of high school. And you won't be a vice president or have a car phone either. You may even have to wear a uniform that doesn't have a Gap label."

"If you think your teacher is tough, wait 'till you get a boss. He doesn't have tenure, so he tends to be a bit edgier."

"Life is not divided into semesters, and you don't get summers off. They expect you to show up every day. For eight hours. And very few employers are interested in helping you find yourself. Do that on your own time."[66]

Real life will not be easy. That's the main message. If you've been around earth for a few years, you know that to be true. Life is not a summer vacation. We've learned this to be reality and it is good. "Life is a test." It's preparing us for the life to come. We must learn our lessons well.

The apostle Peter summarized it well: *"Beloved, do not think it strange concerning the fiery trial which is to try you, as though some strange thing happened to you; but rejoice to the extent that you partake of Christ's sufferings, that when His glory is revealed, you may also be glad with exceeding joy"* (1 Peter 4:12-13).

A long time ago Saint Philip Neri was known for his ability to teach law. Students would come from far and wide to learn from him. He gave this entrance exam to each new student.

"'Why did you come?' he would begin.

"'To study law,' was the standard reply.

"'What will you do when you have studied law?'

"'I will set up my practice.'

"'And after that?'

"'I will get married and have a family.'

"'What then?'

"'I will enjoy my home and my work.'

"'Then what?'

"'Then I will grow older and eventually die.'

"'And after death what then?'

"Thus the great teacher would lead the student to the most certain of life's experiences: '. . . *man is destined to die once, and after that to face judgment'* (Hebrews 9:27). Saint Philip knew that until the student was ready to die, he could not truly be ready to live. Alexander Dumas put it like this: 'If the end be well, all is well.'"[67]

Final graduation has not yet taken place. Life is hard but it's only a test. May we each have ended well when we come to our final graduation – our "promotion to glory", as termed by the Salvation Army.

Thank You Dear Friends!

During one summer season at our church we said our final goodbyes to three of our dear senior friends. The passing of God's saints to their eternal reward is bittersweet. The psalmist describes how God feels about it in the words: *"Precious in the sight of the Lord is the death of his saints"* (Psalm 116:15, KJV). We gathered to remember them, celebrating lives lived amongst us and honoring the legacy each left. We rejoiced in worthy lives lived, clear testimonies of saving faith placed in our Savior, the Lord Jesus Christ, and godly demonstrations of the fruit of the Holy Spirit lived out through them. We reminded ourselves of the forever eternity they were already enjoying with our Heavenly Father and we were challenged to ensure that we too are ready and waiting to one day enter that same destination. That was all good. But, it is bittersweet. Those dear friends are no longer a physical part of our daily lives and we miss them.

Eda suffered for decades, on dialysis, in and out of hospitals for extended periods, enduring discomfort, distress and pain of which most, outside of her family members, were not even aware. Yet she had a sense of humor that would not quit! I've witnessed people of similar ages in like circumstances who became bitter, complaining, negative souls. It would be so easy to do. Not Eda! She looked for and found something light and funny in each day's challenges and shared that with whoever came to visit or assist her. One could not help but love her and leave her presence uplifted. What a model for us all.

Dellarose was one of sweetest ladies I've known. She so wanted to stay active and to keep participating in daily life, making a helpful contribution to our senior ministries in whatever ways she could. As breathing became harder with each day due to the hardening of her lung tissues and as her physical abilities lessened she never quit wanting to assist. Right to the end she used the telephone by her chair to take and pass on messages and stay connected. She started early and planned well for final arrangements and remained cheerful and positive throughout her last two years. She blessed all who came to visit. Thank you dear Dellarose for letting the fragrance of Jesus flow through you to touch us.

Finally, there was John. Father, grandfather, teacher, chaplain, Bible study leader, sometimes sailor – what an interesting man he was. Although in his 80's, he never quit contributing. Meeting with the guys for coffee every week, he didn't say a lot but always added to the conversation. With his wife Irene, each week he drove around to pick up a small group of older ladies, gathering them in one of their homes and leading them through a Bible study. He was remembered at our local large city hospital for the hospital calls he made there for many years as their first volunteer chaplain. He left a legacy of service written in the hearts of his children and grandchildren.

We bless you our friends, now with Jesus. We are reminded to cherish those still here and to make the most of our friendships as we touch each other in our daily lives.

Heaven: Really Real?

Is heaven for real? Do you ever wonder that? True, a heaven to come is the intellectual faith belief of all Christians. It is standard doctrine and an article of faith subscribed to by all who consider themselves true believers. However, as you try to contemplate heaven and what it must be like, do you ever find yourself secretly wondering? Is it really so? How could it possibly be? What must it be like, if really real? Once you go down that questioning trail it seems more and more impossible to believe. How could such a realm exist when there is no evidence of its location in this physical earth-realm, which is all we've known our whole lives?

In those moments of honest doubt, when our minds attempt to wrap themselves around concepts beyond our comprehension, we turn back to the bedrock of our faith: God's Word, the Bible. In it we find descriptions such as this. *9 But as it is written: "Eye has not seen, nor ear heard, Nor have entered into the heart of man the things which God has prepared for those who love Him." 10 But God has revealed them to us through His Spirit. For the Spirit searches all things, yes, the deep things of God* (1 Corinthians 2:9-10, NKJV).

A reality beyond our ability to hear, see or imagine with our limited earthly faculties? Yes, we can identify with that. It is beyond our understanding, yet, we intuitively sense there is more: more than this life. More than what we've already experienced on earth. More beyond! Is it not so? The Spirit of God whispers to our inner beings – that Spirit who has searched the deepest things of Almighty God – he nudges us and we sense deep within that yes, yes there is more to come.

Life has many nostalgic moments that take us back in our memory. A certain smell, a photograph, a song and a pleasant recollection is triggered of a far distant happening in our past. Emotionally we long to go there once again. It is a sweet pain, knowing we cannot – it is gone – but a longing for it remains.

Heaven is like that, only far deeper, far more profound. Deep calls out to deep and we know that we know there is something there calling to us. It is our heart crying out for its true home, longing to be there. Have you felt it? Do you feel it now?

In my lifetime as a pastor I've stood by several people as they prepared to cross from this life to the next and I've even been there when a few made the transition. It is a special and sacred privilege to accompany individuals and their families at such a moment. One such that comes to mind now is of a dear man in his nineties, Abe Friesen, who had walked closely with God all his life and who had a dear, dear family standing by him – Christians, all of them, who too loved their Lord Jesus. What I remember most was Abe's longing to go Home – home to his true Home in Heaven. When he died, there was such a bittersweet joy in that room. I sensed that for a few moments heaven had invaded earth and we knew: we knew that heaven was for real. It is! Do you know that? Are you ready to go there?

φ

LET'S END ... WELL!

Well, fellow baby boomers (and likely a number of older seniors, too), we've come a long way together on our journey into aging. Remember, it's not about old age. It's just about, you! No one else can negotiate my journey for me, nor yours for you. I must set my course, make my choices, and seek to do the very best possible with the tools and opportunities I am given. Same for you. In the words of fellow wayfarer, the Apostle Paul, who probably wrote this when he was in his sixties, *But one thing I do: Forgetting what is behind and straining toward what is ahead, I press on toward the goal to win the prize for which God has called me heavenward in Christ Jesus* (Philippians 3:13-14). We must determine to end well.

In the pages you've read, I hope you've found some inspiration, perhaps at times when you needed it the most, to stretch further, try a little harder, to not give up when you were tempted, and to keep stretching toward the prize God has for us at the end of a life, well-lived. Aging is not for the faint of heart! But it is also a season of life containing many joys, new discoveries and great accomplishments. Let's spur each other on with encouragement. If this volume has been beneficial to you, please pass on the blessing by letting others know about it. One more thing. Let's plan now to stop and have coffee together when we spot each other walking on the streets of gold one day in heaven. See you there!

About the Author

Ross Johnston is a semi-retired pastor living in British Columbia, Canada. In his early years, he worked at a variety of occupations: farmer, student (perpetual!), retail stock boy, geology exploration technician, warehouseman, city pick up and delivery driver, inter-city bus driver, custodian, and residential home construction superintendent, to name a few. He completed four degrees: Th.B., M.R.E., M.Div. and Doctor of Ministry. All of this background prepared him for his major life-time commitment to ministry, working as a senior pastor, associate pastor and representative for several para-church agencies – involvement that spanned over 39 years of service. Service on several ministry boards has broadened his experience. He founded and heads up the service ministry, *Soul Care Sojourners*. He was married in 1971 to Beverley and they have three adult children, one son-in-law and three delightful granddaughters. His ministry to seniors began when he was in his early 20's and has continued up to the present time – a time in which he is now numbered as one of them.

END NOTES

[1] http://www.quotegarden.com/age.html.

[2] *Ibid.*

[3] Duncan Walker (Sept 16, 2004) "Live Fast, Die Old," BBC News site. Retrieved 2007-01-26. Quoted in "Baby Boomers" from *Wikipedia, the free encyclopedia,* at https://en.wikipedia.org/wiki/Baby_boomers.

[4] Eugene Peterson, *The Message: The Bible in Contemporary Language* (Colorado Springs: NavPress, 2002).

[5] Max Lucado, *Cure for the Common Life: Living in Your Sweet Spot* (Nashville: Thomas Nelson, 2008) 68.

[6] Quotations from *The Bible*, unless otherwise indicated, are from the *New International Version (NIV)* translation.

[7] Mendell Taylor, *Every Day With Paul* (Kansas City: Beacon Hill Press of Kansas City, 1978) 253-54.

[8] Randall Arthur, *Wisdom Hunter* (Sisters, OR: Questar Publishers, 1991) 318.

[9] Elizabeth Newehuyse, *Marriage Partnership*, Vol. 7, no. 3.

[10] Richard Bergstrom, Leona Bergstrom, *Third Calling: What are you doing the rest of your life?* (Edmonds, WA: Re-Ignite.net, 2016) Kindle Locations 250-252.

[11] Richard P. Johnson, Johnson Institute: Creative Faith Formation for Boomers and Elders (www.SeniorAdultMinistry.com).

[12] James Houston and Michael Parker, *A Vision for the Aging Church: Renewing Ministry for and by Seniors* (Westmont, IL: IVP Academic, 2011).

[13] Martin A. Janis, *The Joys of Aging* (Nashville: W Publishing Group, 1st ed., 1988)

[14] Ken Dychtwald, *Age Wave*, 1990, 174-75, quoted in Rose, *God's Plan for Significance*, 2006, 5-6.

[15] For information go to http://www.barkerville.ca/.

[16] "Quotable Quotes," *The Reader's Digest* (Pleasantville, N.Y., Vol. 106, No. 637, May, 1975) 136.

[17] J. Allan Petersen, ed. *The Marriage Affair* (Wheaton: Tyndale House Publishers, 1971) 96.

[18] Sydney Martin, *"Thessalonians, Timothy, Titus,"* *Beacon Bible Expositions* (Kansas City: Beacon Hill Press of Kansas City, Vol. 10, 1977) 168-69.

[19] Jim Collins, *Good To Great: Why Some Companies Make the Leap and Others Don't* (New York: Collins / HarperCollinsPublishers, 2001).

[20] Thom S. Rainer, *Breakout Churches: Discover How to Make the Leap* (Grand Rapids: Zondervan, 2005).

[21] Tommy Barnett, *The Power of a Half Hour* (Colorado Springs: Waterbrook Press, 2013).

[22] Chuck Swindoll, *The Finishing Touch: Becoming God's Masterpiece* (Dallas: Word Publishing, 1994) 124-25.

[23] *Ibid.*

[24] E. Stanley Jones, *Abundant Living* (New York: Pillar Books, 1976 [1942]) 344.

[25] Robert H. Schuller, *Self-love* (New York: Jove Publications, Inc., 1969) 108-9.

[26] Lucado, in *Grace for the Moment: More Inspirational Thoughts for Each Day of the Year*, Volume II, Daily calendar (Siloam Springs, AR: DaySpring Cards, Ltd., 2006), August 16.

[27] Quoted in Honor Books, *A Little Devotional Book for Grandparents* (Colorado Springs: Cook Communications, 2003), 312-13.

[28] Robert J. Arnott, *The Minister's Manual (Doran's)* (San Francisco: Harper & Row Publishers, 1971 ed., 1970) 309.

29 Mendell Taylor, *op. cit.*, 226.

30 Charles Colson with Ellen Santilli Vaughn, *The Body: Being Light in Darkness* (Dallas: Word Publishing, 1992) 184.

31 Hebrews 11:4, *King James Version.*

32 E. Stanley Jones, *Growing Spiritually* (London: Hodder and Stoughton, 1954) 276.

33 John White, *Greater Than Riches: Daily Readings to Enrich Your Walk with God* (Downer's Grove: InterVarsity Press, 1992) 114-5. Taken from *Parents In Pain*, 102-3.

34 Al Bryant, ed., *Songs of My Soul: Devotional Thoughts from the Writings of W. Phillip Keller* (Dallas: Word Publishing, 1989) 176-177.

35 Steven P. Wickstrom, *"Acts 27: Shipwrecked in the Storms of Life"* (http://www.spwickstrom.com/acts27/).

36 J. Oswald Sanders, quoted in *Leadership* (Carol Stream, IL.: Christianity Today, Inc., Vol. VII, No. 3, Summer 1986) 86.

37 Leonard Griffith, *God in Man's Experience* (Waco: Word Books, 1968) 32.

38 Vernon Grounds, "Apatheists," *Our Daily Bread* (Grand Rapids: Our Daily Bread Ministries, 2004) June 21.

39 Sarah Young, *Jesus Calling: Enjoying Peace in His Presence* (Nashville: Thomas Nelson, 2004) 54.

40 Lucado, *op. cit., Come Thirsty*, in *Grace for the Moment*, Feb.19

41 Rick Warren, Saddleback Community Church, available at https://store.pastors.com/collections/daring-faith-the-key-to-miracles.

42 Warren Wiersbe, *Wiersbe's Expository Outlines on the New Testament* (QuickVerse digital edition).

43 Laura Hillenbrand, *Unbroken: A World War II Story of Survival, Resilience, and Redemption* (New York: Random House, 2010).

44 Ralph Earle, on Galatians 5:13, *Peloubet's Notes: 1976 September – 1977 August* (Grand Rapids: Baker Book House, 103rd Annual Volume, 1976) 84.

45 James S. Hewett, *Illustrations Unlimited* (Wheaton: Tyndale House Publishers, Inc, 1988), 422, Topic: Prayer, Index: 2816-2841, Date: 7/1996.1402, Title: To Pray Is Human, *Bible Illustrator for Windows: Today's Best Illustrations* (Parsons Technologies, Inc. Ver. 3.0f, 1990-98).

46 William Barclay, *The Gospel of Luke, Rev. ed.,"The Daily Study Bible Series"* (Philadelphia: The Westminster Press, 1975) 203.

47 W. Phillip Keller, *God Is My Delight* (Grand Rapids: Kregel Publications, 1991) 109.

48 John Ortberg, *Everybody's Normal Till You Get to Know Them* (Grand Rapids: Zondervan Publishers, 2003).

49 Lucado, *op. cit., A Cure for the Common Life*, in *Grace for the Moment*, April 24.

50 Robert H. Schuller, in *The Minister's Manual (Doran's)* (San Francisco: Harper & Row Publishers, 1978 ed., 1977) 149.

51 Accessed from https://www.agingcare.com/Articles/bad-behavior-assisted-living-154901.htm.

52 For information go to www.agingcare.com; e.g. https://www.agingcare.com/articles/bad-behavior-by-elderly-parents-138673.htm.

53 Mark Duell, "OAPs Behaving Badly," July 11, 2014, accessed at http://www.dailymail.co.uk/news/article-2683111/OAPs-Behaving-Badly-How-elderly-blowing-pensions-partying-like-teenagers-Tenerife.html.

54 Including Isaiah 22:13, Ecclesiastes 8:15, 1 Corinthians 15:32, and Luke 12:19.

55 John 3:18, *The Message.*

56 *"Laughter, The Best Medicine," Readers Digest* (December, 1977, Vol. III, No. 668) 143.

57 *The Globe and Mail*, Toronto: Thursday, July 19, 2007.

58 Lucado, *op. cit., Next Door Savior*, in *Grace for the Moment*.

59 Gary Smalley and John Trent, *The Blessing* (New York: Pocket Books, 1986) 27.

60 Robert H. Schuller, *Living Positively One Day at a Time*, Vol. 2 for '82 (Garden Grove: Crystal Cathedral Ministries, 1981) October 27.

61 Composed by Henry Smith in 1978.

62 John Maxwell, *Injoy Life Club,* "Growth = Change" (cassette tape, Vol. 5, No. 3).

63 For information go to www.griefshare.org.

64 EMI Music Publishing, 1973.

65 For information go to www.griefshare.org.

66 At http://web.mst.edu/~adekock/Sykes-11-rules.html and other locations.

67 Louis Caldwell, Chapter 2 – "Where to Now?", *After the Tassel Is Moved: Guidelines for High School Graduates* (Grand Rapids: Baker Book House, [1968] 1990, rev. ed.) 22.

Made in the USA
Columbia, SC
27 June 2020